THE LIGHTHOUSE ROUTE

A PERSONAL GUIDE TO THE
SOUTH SHORE OF NOVA SCOTIA

JUDITH COMFORT

NIMBUS
PUBLISHING

Nimbus Publishing Limited
PO Box 9301, Station A
Halifax, Nova Scotia B3K 5N5
(902) 455-4286

Design: Kathy Kaulbach, Halifax
Photos: NS Economic Development & Tourism
Cover photo: Terry James, Lighthouse Photography
Printed and bound in Canada by Best Book Manuf.

Canadian Cataloguing in Publication Data
Comfort, Judith.
Rediscover the Lighthouse Route
Includes bibliographical references.
ISBN 1-55109-106-2
1. Nova Scotia—Guidebooks. I. Title.
FC2345.S68A3 1995   917.16′2044   C95-950078-2
F1039.S68C66 1995

CONTENTS

To me travel writing is a kind of archaeology. Setting out with an open mind, I don't like to dwell on the past. But along the way I keep coming upon the relics, artifacts, and monuments of the past. I have a thousand questions that can only be answered by studying the record, both human and natural.

After driving for half an hour down a deeply rutted gravel road, I come upon a beautifully crafted home, now in a state of silvered disrepair. I wonder why anyone would build this house here in the middle of nowhere.

In Yarmouth I explore two floors of an old fire station full of shiny fire-fighting equipment. Why would anyone go to all the trouble to set up a museum for this cast-off machinery?

Thousands of people flock daily to a barren rock called Peggy's Cove. I want to come to terms with the power of this place.

I feel that I need answers to these questions before I can truly understand what I am seeing while travelling many miles up and down this shore. Sometimes, however, I find there are no answers to be had. I am content, then, to discover that others share my own sense of wonder.

For answers I have always counted on the great storehouses of the human record—libraries. I find friends, teachers, and mentors in the printed word. I want an explanation for the phenomenon at Blue Rocks and find my answer in Albert E. Roland's *Geological Background and Physiography of Nova Scotia.* Standing on a sand beach watching waves crashing at my feet, I am overwhelmed, not only by the power of nature, but also by my inability to describe what I am witnessing. I look to Roland and he gives me the vocabulary.

I have always felt uneasy driving through the acres and acres of barrens and bog in Shelburne and Yarmouth counties. I am inspired to see the beauty of the bog as lovingly described in John Erskine's *In Forest and Field.*

I could never understand why my side of the harbour is covered with boulders and stunted spruce while the other side is blanketed with lush fields and hardwood hills. Then I find the voice of Ralph S. Johnson and his history of what "man hath wrought" on the forests of this province.

At the library I also discover Mather Byles DesBrisay who would have been a neighbour of mine 100 years ago. His chatty, enthusiastic *History of Lunenburg County* makes me sorry to have been born out of his time. He must have been a fascinating man. He is an invaluable resource in my understanding of modern Lunenburg County. My present resonates with his past.

And I am indebted to Clara Dennis who travelled the same path as me in 1934 capturing the textures of people's domestic lives missing from more formal histories of Nova Scotia.

This book was not written to promote anything. I have tried to describe the most interesting and compelling aspects of the South Shore. I wish I had been mandated to write an encyclopedia. As an archaeologist, I know that I have barely scratched the surface. This book is a personal guide to a land I have come to feel very deeply about over the last twenty years.

Judith Comfort
Port Medway, Nova Scotia
October, 1994

HALIFAX AREA

We're in Halifax and we want to get out of the city to explore the countryside. This is not always easy to do. While there is a large land mass between St. Margaret's Bay and Halifax Harbour—almost within spitting distance of the largest city in the Maritimes—it is virtually inaccessible. Few gravel roads even penetrate the interior of the peninsula. This intimidating wilderness historically has had little to offer humans. There was not enough soil for farming and what forest was there has been burned repeatedly and is slow to heal itself. But it is a fascinating region nonetheless. Much of it is Crown land, while 5,664 hectares (2,293 acres) near Terence Bay has been nominated for Protected Area status by the provincial government. This landscape is a representative example of the Pennant Coastal Granite Barrens.

Looking for a day's excursion we study the map for a loop around the peninsula. In 200 years of settlement road builders have never succeeded in connecting all the tiny settlements along the shore. We follow two smaller loops instead.

HALIFAX TO CRYSTAL CRESCENT BEACH

DIRECTIONS

Starting at the Armdale Rotary proceed along Route 253 to Purcells Cove following the southern shore of the Northwest Arm. Continue to Herring Cove and turn left on Route 349. This road follows the general shoreline of Halifax Harbour to Sambro. At Sambro turn left and follow the signs to

Crystal Crescent Provincial Park. Leaving Sambro return to Halifax through Harrietsfield on Route 306.

To explore the Halifax area shoreline we head out for Route 349. People say it's not as consistently scenic as it used to be. Much of the view is now grown over with shrubbery or supplanted by development. We can understand why people have taken up the shore side of the road and built homes perched on the cliffs overlooking Halifax Harbour and Channel. The rhythm of ocean swells outside the bedroom window and the stark beauty of the barrens would help calm even the most stressed office worker at the end of the day.

Nature still has the upper hand here. For the same reason this road is a healthy Sunday excursion for us.

The feel of the road is much more suburban than rural and there are inland stretches of scrub and not much else. The tiny villages on the very edge of storm-lashed rocks are intriguing. We like to get out of the car and explore them on foot.

YORK REDOUBT

Strange but true: twentieth-century picnickers have a lot in common with eighteenth-century military strategists. Both require a truly extraordinary view of Halifax Harbour—a vantage point so high and commanding that a ship simply cannot pass in or out without being noticed. The observer may be a semaphore operator in the company of Prince Edward, Duke of Kent (and commander in chief at Halifax in 1796), an anti-submarine officer during the Second World War, or a small child who has lost interest in a peanut butter

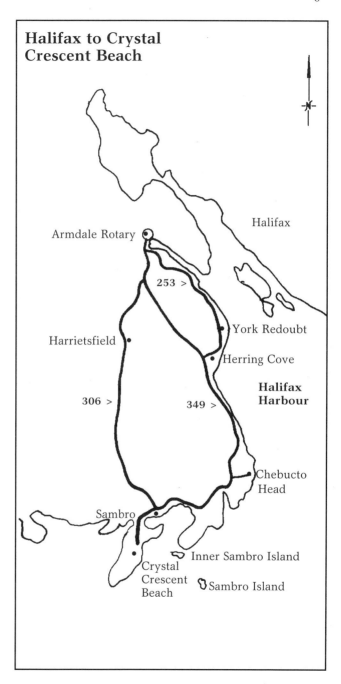

Halifax to Crystal Crescent Beach

Halifax

Armdale Rotary

253 >

York Redoubt

Harrietsfield

Herring Cove

Halifax Harbour

306 >

349 >

Chebucto Head

Sambro

Inner Sambro Island

Crystal Crescent Beach

Sambro Island

sandwich while watching a three story-high container ship float by.

York Redoubt is an important reminder that Halifax was once a garrison town. The 200-year-old fortification is a national historic site complete with ramparts and massive muzzle-bash loading guns capable of firing 256-pound shells (with the help of nine men).

History aside, energetic children love running up and down the grassy mounds of York Redoubt and creeping through the dank castle-like stone passageway deep into the bowels of the hill.

Halifax Harbour at York Redoubt

Herring Cove is a tiny fishing village. Crossing the bridge over the inlet we glance seaward. Stilted buildings perched on wharves on both sides of the "arm" make classic subject matter for painters and photographers. Just outside this placid sanctuary the coastline is treacherous. The lighthouse is situated at Tribune Head, where in 1797 H.M.S. *Tribune* sank on the rocks, taking 240 men, women, and children down with her. Twelve people survived thanks to the bravery of a thirteen-year-old boy named Joe Cracker who braved stormy seas in a rowboat to pick them off the wreckage. Interestingly, the lighthouse wasn't built until 1886.

At Bear Cove we notice a break in the trees and a blue wink of water beckons us to stop. We follow a well-trodden path between two old stone walls to a miniature cove. After the high bluffs of York Redoubt we welcome the opportunity to rest at sea level. The rocky beach is framed by small bluffs with grassy knolls. We're sure that generations of picnickers have been thrilled with this spot.

CHEBUCTO HEAD

At Duncan's Cove Road we ignore the cul-de-sac sign and forge ahead towards Chebucto Head. Chebucto marks the entrance to Halifax Harbour. The name is derived from the Mi'kmaq word "Chebookt," which translated aptly describes Nova Scotia's "chief harbour." The stark terrain and spectacular view have attracted residents who have built expensive homes bunkered into the rocks. Perhaps the sight of whales from the top of this hill compensates for the lack of vegetation.

A sign at the entrance to the Chebucto Light reads, "Caution, Visitors Enter at their own Risk. The Government of Canada assumes no liability for damage to person or property on these premises." The deep potholes in the road might well do damage to our property—our car. Yet another sign further explains the government's concern for our well being. "Fog horn starts automatically. Hearing protection required beyond this point." We are amused, but probably only because it's a glorious bright day. Nearby stands a curious assortment of towers topped with spinning mechanical devices—part of the Chebucto Head Remote Radar and Fog Alarm Site. From this (41.4 metre/136-foot) vantage we can see up Halifax Harbour as well as far out to sea. No land in sight. This is the essence of the wide-open North Atlantic.

CRYSTAL CRESCENT BEACH PROVINCIAL PARK

We continue on through barrens and small villages. We make a note to return to Sambro Harbour and explore it by sea kayak. At a fork in the road, (instead of returning on Route 306 towards Harrietsfield and Halifax) we turn left towards Coote Cove (its old name) or Crystal Crescent Beach Provincial Park as it's called now. We drive past a futuristic complex of satellite dishes, NO TRESPASSING signs, communication towers, chain link fences, and a huge, grim parking lot. And then we see the beach—a rare jewel in this bleak landscape: vulnerable heaps of white sand precariously held by a clutch of marram grass, bordered by a ruffle of frothy surf.

Two islands are visible: Inner Sambro (a corruption of the original French word, *Sesambre,* an island near St. Malo) and further out Sambro, a rocky foundation for the oldest active lighthouse on the east coast of Canada. It has stood watch over all who have passed through Halifax Harbour since 1758. The original lighthouse was a stone tower with a whale-oil lantern on top. It was replaced in 1906 by an octagonal stone and concrete tower. The light source was upgraded to a petroleum vapour incandescent burner with an efficient bull's-eye lens. This lens is now a permanent fixture in the entrance of the Nova Scotia Museum in Halifax.

With the dense fog that hovers over the mouth of the harbour it is obvious why mariners needed more than visual clues to keep them on course. Rear Admiral Hugh F. Pullen describes the evolution of foghorns in his book *The Sea Road to Halifax.* In the beginning sailors would simply shoot off guns to alert lighthouse keepers of their presence. The keepers responded in kind. In 1865 the government of Nova Scotia installed a Daboll fog trumpet, a reed horn that proved unreliable, then reverted to a battery of 24-pound guns that were fired in response to steamer whistles of the day. Sambro eventually got its own steam fog whistle, but in 1891 the whole sound system was moved to Chebucto Head. There they used bomb rockets, acetylene guns, and diaphone horns. Finally, in 1972, modern foghorns were returned to Sambro Island.

WHITES LAKE TO UPPER TANTALLON

DIRECTIONS

Leave Halifax on Route 103 west. Continue to Exit 2 at Beechville and follow Route 333 through Whites Lake and Peggy's Cove. Continue on Route 333 following the eastern shore of St. Margaret's Bay to Upper Tantallon. To return to Halifax, turn right on Route 3 east. To continue the scenic tour turn left on Route 3 west to Hubbards.
This drive is more destination than drive. It's mostly about getting to Peggy's Cove. The 333 is a nondescript route until Whites Lake

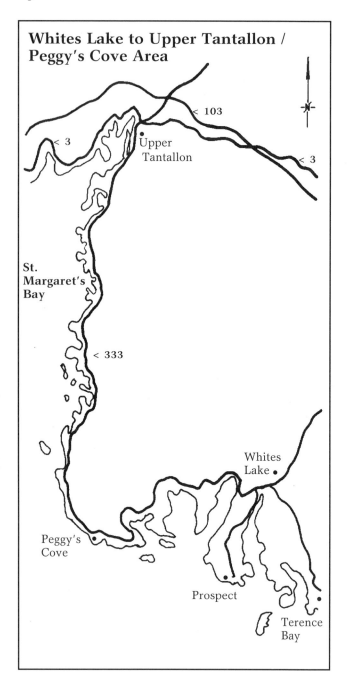

Whites Lake to Upper Tantallon / Peggy's Cove Area

< 103

< 3

Upper
Tantallon

< 3

St.
Margaret's
Bay

< 333

Whites
Lake ●

Peggy's
Cove

Prospect

Terence
Bay

where the traveller can choose the road to
Terence Bay, or Prospect, or to continue on
straight to Peggy's Cove. Terence Bay is a
community perched on the rocks and Pennant
Barrens. In spite of being so close to a large
metro area, it has the ambiance of a Newfoundland outport. Lower Prospect is the site
of a major shipwreck. In 1873 the SS *Atlantic*
struck Meaghers (Marrs) Island taking 562
people down with it. Two hundred and sev-
enty-seven of them are buried here. The 2.5-
kilometre (4-mile) drive to Prospect offers
little in the way of a view, but the pictur-
esque village nestled into the boulders at sea
level is well worth the side trip.

Prospect

THE PEGGY'S COVE AREA

Driving down the peninsula we are struck by
the changing shades of green. As we get
closer to the sea, healthy mixed forest gives
way to scrubby spruce hummocks. Trees
have a harder time making a go of it next to
the open ocean. The temperature drops sud-
denly, a hazy fog hovers, and the wind stiff-
ens. This is typical of Nova Scotia's indented

coastline, but Peggy's Cove is different. Here, trees aren't merely stunted—they're nonexistent. There is a green fuzz on the surface, but clearly what has dominion over this landscape is that which is normally hidden—the substrata, the bedrock. Devonian granite, a mixture of quartz, feldspar, mica, and hornblende, has heaved its way to the surface. At the water's edge, waves have quarried out steps in the naturally jointed material. Scored into the surface like the markings on a primate palm are a crisscross of grooved lines.

Most astonishing are the thousands of freestanding rocks and boulders sitting like carefully placed sculptures or tombstones on

Erratics at Peggy's Cove

the bulging bedrock. They're called "erratics"—rocks that were picked up hundreds of miles from here by the slow but relentlessly grinding mantles of ice during the last ice age. They were dropped where we see them after the mammoth force was reduced to a puddle.

Erratics are common all over Nova Scotia. We've come across them in the woods, covered by a carpet of moss, perhaps with a tree sprouting out of a crevice. But here, there is little soil and vegetation to mask their desolate appearance.

That's not to suggest that life does not abound in the bog amidst the rocks. Generations of fires have repeatedly upset the soil and the barren is nature's first step in forgiving. Sphagnum mosses, sedges, blueberries, and bracken fern all thrive. The macabre queen of the bog is the pitcher-plant (*Sarracenia purpurea*). Its tall mahogany and pink flowers rise above four-lipped pitcher-shaped leaves that collect rain water. Non-suspecting insects are attracted to the coloured lip, venture down into the plant and are trapped by the stiff downward pointing hairs. They drown and after bacterial and enzyme breakdown are digested by the carnivorous plant.

THE TOWN OF PEGGY'S COVE

Rather than heading directly to the restaurant and lighthouse we park in the provincial parking lot and walk the winding road through the village to the rocks. Blue and poppy-red fishing boats are tied to the wharf in the tiny cove. Petunias spill out of a cast-iron pot next to the gift shop. Inside we linger over the vast assortment of tourist memorabilia: Peggy's Cove baseball caps, Peggy's

Cove bone china mugs, Peggy's Cove Christmas ornaments.

We examine the details of William DeGarthe's memorial sculpture to fishermen, chiselled out of a 30-metre (100-foot) granite outcropping next to his house. The monumental work includes a company of thirty-two fishermen, their wives and children, a guardian angel with her wings outspread, and the legendary "Peggy," the namesake of the village. There's talk that cars may be banned from the village, and that would be a good thing. An automobile is a bull in china shop here.

Peggy's Cove Lighthouse and rocks

THE ROCKS AT PEGGY'S COVE

It's hard to approach this almost iconic landscape without preconceptions. We steel ourselves for a stampede of fellow tourists. Our cynicism is understandable. (The name Peggy's Cove rolls off travel agents' tongues as easily as Niagara Falls.) But our negative feelings wash away upon first sight. Even though the rocks are swarmed with people, this place has little to do with human beings. Yet it all feels so familiar.

In spite of the powerfully intimidating waves that rise and froth and cascade and break before us, we feel safe. We watch them building far offshore; we follow the swells as they crash on the granite face. Any one of those waves might quite dispassionately sweep us off our feet into the briny maelstrom. What do we feel? Is it fear, awe, or just the sound of our own heartbeat: not the gentle pat, pat of a pulse—but the whoosh and slosh of salty red through veins and arteries. We feel the muffled air pushing its way past our eardrums more than we hear it. Looking out to sea our eyes rest at infinity. We feel a visceral connection to those wild, yet wonderfully predictable waves. Amidst the turbulence, we feel secure.

There are hundreds of us: stretched out absorbing the sun's radiant warmth; clowning for a group photo; hunched dangerously close to the dark wet edges, totally mesmerized. Surprisingly we don't mind. This 415-million-year-old rock seems able to diminish and absorb the presence of any number of humans. Leaving Peggy's Cove behind we drive to Route 103 through a series of former fishing villages now inhabited mostly by people who work in the city. The water is visible in flashes, much of the shoreline hidden behind privately owned peninsulas. We are happy to see more lush vegetation as we get closer to the head of the bay.

UPPER TANTALLON TO HUBBARDS

DIRECTIONS

Leave Halifax on Route 103 west. Continue to Exit 5, and turn left toward Upper Tantallon. Proceed to the intersection of Route 3 and turn right on Route 3 west to Hubbards.

At Upper Tantallon we reach the northeastern corner of St. Margaret's Bay and turn west towards Hubbards. This road affords dramatic views of the gentle head of the bay from on high. This ledge alongside Dauphinee Mountain reaches heights of 91 metres (300 feet). The intimate shoreline is very wooded and lake-like. Lovely homes are nestled in the hardwoods overlooking tiny inlets, while yachts anchored close by bob in the waves. Wood, Strawberry, Potato, and Croucher islands complete the marine panorama. It's hard to decide which of these villages is prettier: Head of St. Margarets, Boutiliers Point, Ingramport, or Black Point.

Just past Upper Tantallon at French Village (not to be confused with the French Village near Seabright) is the Old Annapolis Road Hiking Trail. An 8-kilometre (5-mile) drive takes visitors to the "pocket wilderness"—one of several set aside for the public by the Bowater Mersey Paper Company. The trails wend their way through uncut and cut-over lands to give visitors a sample of modern forest "management." Part of the trail follows an ancient route that was cut after the War of 1812 to encourage settlement in the interior of the province.

We take Conrads Road behind Queensland Beach and happily leave the car.

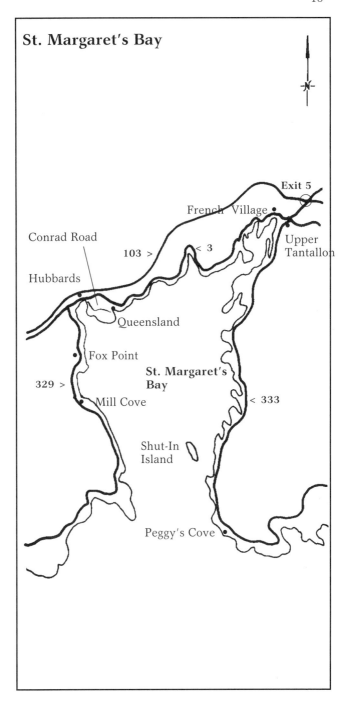

St. Margaret's Bay

-N-

Exit 5

French Village

Upper Tantallon

Conrad Road

103 >

< 3

Hubbards

Queensland

Fox Point

St. Margaret's Bay

329 >

< 333

Mill Cove

Shut-In Island

Peggy's Cove

The orange-tinged sands reflect the hue of the smooth granite rocks behind them. This is the sheltered top of St. Margaret's Bay and the swimming is far more comfortable here than at the mouth of the bay, close to Peggy's Cove. A sand spit separates Queensland Lake from the salt water and we wish we could stay awhile in one of the small cottages next to the lake. We'd like to row out and visit the ducks. Instead, we pile into the car and drive, driving across the back of the beach to a pretty side road that takes us through a sleepy wood to Hubbards.

Beach at Queensland

Hubbards is a quaint resort community that feels almost abandoned ten months of the year. It has an incongruous mix of historic buildings (the lovely Dauphinee Inn and gothic-style St. Luke's Anglican Church), and tourist cabins and motels. It sits at the outer rim of a comfortable commute from the city and so has been adopted by a few fortunate people. In the little cove we watch an osprey fishing unselfconsciously, seemingly suspended in mid-flight. Dauphinees Beach at the end of the road is accessible primarily through the Shore Club and a private campground.

THE ASPOTOGAN PENINSULA

DIRECTIONS

Leave Hubbards on Route 3 west. Take Route 329 to Fox Point, Mill Cove, and Aspotogan. Continue on Route 329, which follows the shore of the Aspotogan Peninsula and returns to Route 3 at East River. To return to Route 103, turn left at Route 3, cross the East River and proceed to the junction of Route 3 and Route 103 at Exit 7.

From Halifax take Route 103 west to Exit 6. Turn left at Route 3 toward Hubbards then right on Route 329 to Fox Point, Mill Cove, and Aspotogan. Continue on Route 329 which follows the shore of the Aspotogan Peninsula and returns to Route 3 at East River. To return to Route 103, turn left at Route 3, cross the East River and proceed to the junction of Route 3 and Route 103 at Exit 7.

Like the peninsula between Halifax Harbour and St. Margaret's Bay, the Aspotogan Peninsula (between St. Margaret's Bay and Mahone Bay) is largely uninhabited except along the seacoast. Luckily for travellers, a road connects these shore communities. We are intrigued as we set out on this journey because this peninsula boasts the highest vantage on the South Shore—Aspotogan Mountain.

Leaving Route 3 for Route 329, we follow Hubbards Cove. Fish nets drying on the metal guard rails tell us that we've left the resort area behind us. At Fox Point we stop at a little beach to stretch our legs and stare over the glistening expanse of St. Margaret's Bay. The Aspotogan Peninsula stretches off into the horizon on our right.

At The Ledge a huge primeval turtle rises out of the waves across the harbour. It is Shut-In Island, which we saw close-up from the Hacketts Cove side of the bay. With trees long since burnt off it looks bleak and naked.

Northwest Cove and Aspotogan are typical fishing villages. Red, yellow, and blue boats bob next to pewter-coloured wharves. Weathered stores with small-paned windows are remarkably intact. Quaint enough for a movie set? Yes indeed. In 1956 a film crew from the J. Arthur Rank Organization arrived here to film *High Tide at Noon.* Apparently they transformed the town of 100 overnight and put the villagers on the payroll for a "solid fortnight."

The road meanders high above the sea. Aspotogan Mountain ascends to its full height a mile inland. Serious hikers would do well to seek out a woods path that cuts through the back country to the 160-metre (525-foot) top. It is reputed to be a huge chunk of slate 3 kilometres (1.9 miles) long and less than 1 kilometre wide. It has resisted the stresses of time, while the area around it has been eroded down to an average altitude of only 80 metres (262 feet). For the geologically curious: this is called a "monadnock."

Mather Byles DesBrisay wrote in 1895 that Aspotogan was a noted landmark to navigators and on a clear day it could be seen from many parts of the county "with the beautiful blue distance tint so admired by artists."

Coming into Bayswater, we catch a glimpse of the Peggy's Cove Light across the way. The harbour is littered with fragments of gravel islands and ledges. The beach here is a gift of those disintegrating islands. The

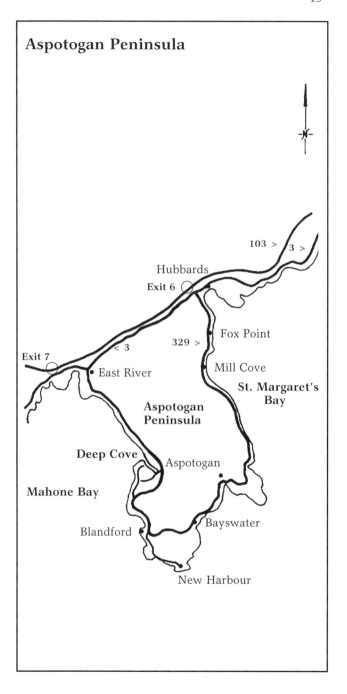

Aspotogan Peninsula

Hubbards
Exit 6

103 > 3 >

Fox Point

< 3   329 >

Exit 7

East River   Mill Cove

St. Margaret's
Bay

Aspotogan
Peninsula

Deep Cove
Aspotogan

Mahone Bay

Bayswater

Blandford

New Harbour

provincial picnic park across the street is situated on the more sedate Bayswater Pond but we prefer the wild whitecaps.

After barrens and woods it is a surprise to come out of the trees into mown fields. Blandford is a village of snug old Cape Cod homes overlooking the dozens of offshore islands in Mahone Bay. We crave more open ocean and take a dead-end diversion, turning left towards New Harbour. Covey's Auto Recyclers has the most spectacular view of any junkyard on this shore—maybe of any used-car graveyard in North America—with a thrilling view of East Ironbound, Little Tancook and Big Tancook islands. We follow the craggy shoreline speckled with cormorants and herons and don't turn around until we reach the wreckage of a fish plant.

Returning to Blandford we take a little diversion in Upper Blandford sticking to the shoreline (turning left to Gates Cove). From here we gain a different perspective of the Chester Islands. At the end of the road we turn around and turn left at a gravel road that brings us back to the main road at a dramatic junction. Here Deep Cove stretches inland to touch the steep reddish rock face of Deep Cove/Aspotogan Mountain.

DEEP COVE

Deep Cove is a narrow, mile-long finger of the sea, a natural extension of a fault in the earth's crust. We long for an unobstructed view up the cove but have to be satisfied with a quick snapshot as we drive over the bridge. A developer is advertising lots for sale, and we can't resist the opportunity for a closer look. What an enchanted wood! Thousands of rocks, some the size of small cars have come to rest on the steeply inclined forest floor. They were once part of the sheer rock face but during a geologic cataclysm tumbled down to where they now rest. A green moss carpet makes a common denominator of the boulders and tree stumps. All become a soft bedding for ferns. All the water off the mountain gushes through here feeding the darkly shaded forest, which has more in common with the great coal swamps of the Paleozoic era than the manicured hills of Blandford.

GRAVES ISLAND PROVINCIAL PARK, EAST CHESTER

DIRECTIONS

Leave Halifax on Route 103 west. Take Exit 7 at East River and turn right on Route 3 west to East Chester.

Islands are usually places we long for from a distance, but here is Graves Island, within kissing distance of the mainland. A quick run across the causeway and we're on an island. Thirty years ago an enlightened provincial government had the good sense to preserve this island dream for the future.

Several cars are parked at the picnic-park entrance. The drivers sit behind the wheel just staring out at the pastoral beauty of Scotch Cove and the unfolding hills. Two dozen tables provide lots of room for family outings. (The rampart-like monkey bars and house-high slide particularly impress the children.)

The camping park is not for those seeking the rough and tumble bush. Sleeping under the stars on Graves Island feels more like a wondrous but very safe first time out in the

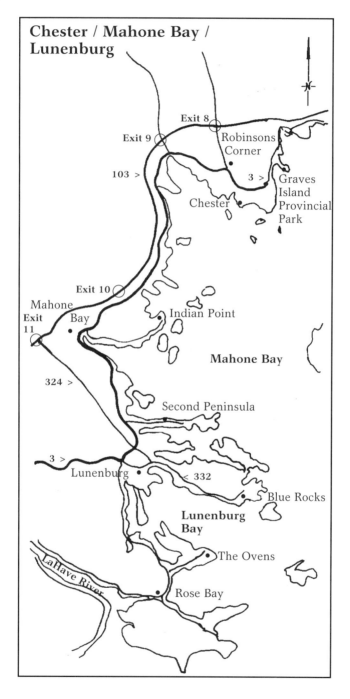

Chester / Mahone Bay / Lunenburg

Exit 8

Exit 9

Robinsons
Corner

103 >

3 >

Graves
Island
Provincial
Park

Chester

Exit 10

Mahone
Bay

Exit
11

Indian Point

Mahone Bay

324 >

Second Peninsula

3 >

Lunenburg

< 332

Blue Rocks

Lunenburg
Bay

LaHave River

The Ovens

Rose Bay

back yard. But what a back yard—a 45-hectare (111-acre) island; a farmer's field mowed to soft green grass. The island was settled in the 1700s by German settlers named "Graff" or "Graeff." The name was Anglicized into Graves and the island remained continuously inhabited until the land was (unfortunately for the owners) expropriated for the park.

There are also some wooded sites and groomed hiking trails. The best camping sites are numbers twenty through twenty-three with a view out to sea—the islands and the Aspotogan Peninsula. We wish we'd brought binoculars. This shoreline on the northeast side of Mahone Bay is unusually straight, having been formed by a fault in the earth's crust. We can see the beige cliffs where the earth has cracked and slipped down. Behind them rises the blue of Aspotogan Mountain.

CHESTER

DIRECTIONS

Leave Halifax on Route 103 west. Take Exit 7 at East River and turn right on Route 3 west to Chester.

Leave Yarmouth on Route 103 east to Exit 8. Turn right on Route 14 south to Robinsons Corner. Turn left on Route 3 east to Chester.

We get confused driving around Chester, but never actually get lost because the old town plot is located on a sack-shaped peninsula between twin harbours: Front and Back. We drive in circles until we get where we want to go. Running across the top of the peninsula is Route 3 (also called North Street). The streets have been laid out in a very logical grid, by the Crown surveyor, and given suitably regal names like King, Queen, and Duke. The one anomaly is a road along the water called Valley Road, which turns into Water Street.

Beyond the confines of the old town, newer development stretches up to Robinsons Corner and East Chester. Elegant residential properties on dead-end roads dot the shoreline. The yacht club is south of the town near a causeway that connects the mainland to a privately owned island called The Peninsula.

Chester

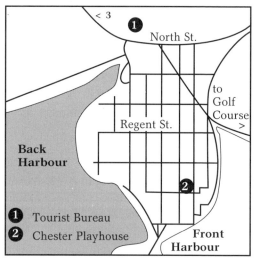

COMMERCIAL CHESTER

Because of the influx of summer people, Chester has some of the commercial advantages not found in similar Maritime towns with a winter population of 1,250: things like a choice of restaurants. Some people prefer an elegant meal in front of a fire in a warmly paneled nineteenth-century mansion. Others like to sit outside a European-style bakery in the sunshine and nibble on a luscious blue-

berry tart. Takeout here means dropping into
a local funky restaurant at 10 p.m. to pick up
a slice of chocolate truffle cake to go with a video.

And there is live theatre. The Chester
Playhouse pulls out all the stops during its
summer festival producing almost fifty shows
in two months. The small, intimate 176-seat
venue presents professional plays (such as *A
Closer Walk with Patsy Cline, Leacock Speaks*),
featuring professional performers, such as
Garnet Rogers, Catherine McKinnon, and
Don Harron, as well as community produc-
tions and those of the Chester Summer School
Theatre.

We like to wander down to the Victorian
pagoda-style bandstand for a performance of
the Chester Brass. This band (originally called
the First Chester Coronet Band) has been en-
tertaining since 1873. It is patterned after the
traditional British brass band with brass and
percussion but no woodwinds. The band
plays an eclectic mix of Bach, Salvation Army
hymns, and Broadway scores—against a back-
drop of sailboats and wooded islands.

CHESTER ISLANDS

Chester is all about the islands: Big and Little
Gooseberry, Clay, Quaker, Meisners, Woody,
Mark, Mountain, Saddle, Snake. Some rise
out of the water like great high-sided beasts
with green brush cuts. Others are low and
slouching rubble-bellied creatures. Sometimes
they are shrouded in mist, other times they
appear crystal clear and close enough to
touch. But it is difficult to find a good vantage
point from the mainland because much of
Chester is hidden in trees on private property.
Driving down shore lanes, we see the backs

of opulent homes, and only through a break in the shrubbery do we get a glimmer of what is seen out their front windows.

CHESTER RACE WEEK

In this sailors' paradise we are handicapped without a boat. Luckily there are boat cruises and charters and a ferry boat to Tancook Island. Chester Race Week is the time when tourists, residents, summer people, yachtsmen, and landlubbers celebrate the sailing culture of Chester.

The first sailing races were held around 1885 when the sailboat was not the pleasure

Chester Race Week, Chester

craft of the wealthy but a workhorse and a basic means of transportation. Shipbuilding in Lunenburg County was a fine art, and there was a good-natured rivalry between different communities. (Which was better, the Little Tancook sloop or the Big Tancook whaler?) A race seemed the logical way to resolve the argument. The competitors in the races of those days were sailors who built their own boats and made their own sails. Local merchants put up prizes such as a 100-pound sack of sugar. About 1894, the summer people started to settle in and the first yachts built solely for pleasure became a factor in the race.

In the summer the sleepy little village of Chester becomes livelier, but during Chester Race Week the town absolutely hums. A warm glow emanates from homes and restaurants. Laughter and music is heard in the streets, posh automobiles with foreign license plates roll up and down the narrow streets. The perfect warm summer evenings never get muggy. There are always lovely cool breezes off the water.

During the brightness of day the blue harbour is filled with a carnival of sails. Crowds stream down to the yacht club to ogle the incoming and outgoing sloops, cutters, ketches, and schooners,—boats from as far away as the Virgin Islands.

CHESTER GOLF COURSE

It would be worth taking up the sport just for the view from the Chester Golf Course. With such magnificent distractions as the bay, islands, and a procession of boats, including the Tancook ferry, it's amazing that anyone can keep their eye on the ball! This mature course is described as "challenging." The original nine-hole course has been recently expanded to eighteen holes. The clubhouse is a remodelled Cape-style farmhouse that serves delicious sandwiches out on the verandah. No kidding, it's best to plan a game to coincide with Chester Race Week.

MAHONE BAY

DIRECTIONS

Leave Halifax on Route 103 west. Take Exit 10 at Oakland and turn right on Route 3 west to Mahone Bay.

Leave Yarmouth on Route 103 east to Exit 11 at Blockhouse. Turn right on Route 324 south toward Lunenburg, then left on Route 325 east to Mahone Bay.

Eleven hundred fortunate people live in Mahone Bay. This small town of gracious homes, weeping willows, and comfortable country lanes, is a place where many long to settle down. It would be easy to relax into the porch swing on the verandah of one of the gingerbread houses or to curl up like that cat in the window seat of an upstairs dormer.

Situated at the head of an extraordinary harbour, the sheltered inlet of Mahone Bay is

Mahone Bay placid enough to allow perfect mirror images of three church spires. The reflections shimmer as

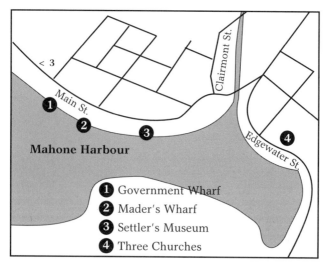

Mahone Harbour

❶ Government Wharf
❷ Mader's Wharf
❸ Settler's Museum
❹ Three Churches

a great blue heron breaks the surface of the water or a billowy sailboat tacks by. Mahone Bay learned before other towns to capitalize on its loveliness and many city dweller's ideal Sunday escape is to this town. Mahone Bay's commercial success can be measured by the fact that in spite of its size there actually are traffic jams in summer.

We prefer to shop in Mahone Bay at Christmas. Bill's Store is a must because it has

one of the best toy departments in the province. This classic five and dime store has been in business for forty years and sells everything from baby's booties to cookie jars shaped like ducks in yellow slickers. We enjoy the old-fashioned displays, the Christmas fabrics, and Indian-crafted leather moccasins. Children like to shake the snow-filled glass globes, and wind up all the music boxes.

Three Churches, Mahone Bay

There are dozens of one-of-a-kind stores in Mahone Bay, good solid businesses with established artisans who have paid their dues here for a decade or more. Vicki Lynn Bardon of Suttles and Seawinds has a special eye for selecting fabric from all over the world and creating collages that startle and delight. Amos Pewterers creates tiny sand-dollar earrings. The Teazer gift shop has been in business for thirty years and has been an anchor store for the area—amongst the first to make Nova Scotia crafts available to tourists, including Cheticamp hooking, quilts, and folk art. And there are all kinds of bright newcomers: Jamie Skoczylas of Wind Rose specializes in custom-made European linens and lace.

Add to this antique stores, a bookstore, art galleries, an English pub, the Tingle Bridge Tea House, and Jack and Katherine Sorenson's cooking genius at the Innlet Cafe—the choices are quite remarkable.

The Mahone Bay Founders Society, devoted to preserving local history, operates the Mahone Bay Settler's Museum at 578 Main Street. Of particular interest is the Ceramic Gallery featuring pieces from the collection of Percy Inglis who in the 1930s operated the family store specializing in fine English china (this was situated in the building now owned by Suttles and Seawinds). His personal collections included tableware of the eighteenth and early nineteenth century: cream ware, pearlware, lustre ware, iron stone, and porcelain.

For an informative guide to the architectural delights of Mahone Bay we refer to an excellent pamphlet titled *3 Walking Tours of Mahone Bay* published by the Founders Society. They offer a house tour each year that allows the curious to peek inside historic homes.

THE MAHONE BAY WOODEN BOAT FESTIVAL

The Mahone Bay Wooden Boat Festival brings together a community of people whose

interest, occupation, and passion is wooden
boats. It is not just a historical, nostalgic retro-
spective but a celebration of a living craft. For
five days, the harbour is literally full of boats.
The nerve centre of the festival is the government wharf where painstakingly well-crafted
boats are displayed. There are tours (by boat
of course) to local boat yards to visit master
shipwrights and see their works in progress.
Workshops and demonstrations are offered on
such subjects as sail making, canoe building,
wood-epoxy laminating, hull fitting, knot ty-
ing, and model-boat building. There are five
days of entertainment including races, fireworks, sidewalk painting, and treasure hunts.
A highlight of the festival is the Parade of Sail.
Spectators line up along the government wharf

and shoreline to watch a flotilla of vessels.
Hundreds of boats of every size and descrip-
tion drift by while spirited commentary is
broadcast over the loudspeakers.

The Wooden Boat Festival, Mahone Bay

A triathlon is held simultaneously with
the wooden boat festival. Last year athletes
competed along a 48.5 kilometre (30-mile)
route comprised of 25 kilometres (15.5 miles)
cycling, 12.5 kilometres (7.8 miles) running
and 11 kilometres (6.8 miles) of kayaking.

MAHONE BAY TO INDIAN POINT

DIRECTIONS

Leave Mahone Bay on Route 3 east. Turn right at the head of the bay, just past Kedy's Landing following the road along the northern shore of Mahone Bay to Indian Point.

For a postcard view of Mahone Bay we head up the northern side of the bay towards Indian Point. A dozen yachts are anchored here and their masts are mirrored, like the churches steeples, on the placid water. Closer to Indian Point pleasure crafts are no longer in the majority. Dories and Cape Island boats are moored to wharves and cribbing. Our view encompasses a dozen islands. The list of names, read aloud, sounds like the passenger list of the ships that brought German settlers to this harbour: Ernst, Zwicker, Strum, Kaulbeck, and Rafuse. One small island retains its German name—Klungemache Island. Translated roughly it means, "to make a sound." We wonder what sound inspired this name: the howling wind, sizzling beach pebbles, or something supernatural?

The road ends at Indian Point, a pleasant, well-tended farming and fishing community. We notice balconies and skylights on the fish sheds, marigolds and Adirondack chairs on the wharves. The community is quaint and pretty, if a bit gentrified. Mather Byles DesBrisay comments that there was an Indian settlement and a burial ground at Indian Point, the last burial having taken place around 1845.

SECOND PENINSULA

DIRECTIONS

Leave Mahone Bay on Route 3 west toward Lunenburg. Turn left at the road to Second Peninsula.

Leave Lunenburg on Route 3 east toward Mahone Bay. Turn right at the road to Second Peninsula.

Second Peninsula is a scenic drive and also a picnic destination. The entrance to this luxuriously wooded 6.9 kilometre (5-mile) digit of land is a short 1.6 kilometres (1 mile) north of Lunenburg and about 5.5 kilometres (4 miles) southeast of Mahone Bay. The road is essential Lunenburg County—a quilt of greens: rugged dark-olive woods patched next to grass-green hills and a cabbage field of bluish-green. Well-groomed whale-back farms are salt and peppered with black and white cows. And there is water wherever we turn. The road follows the margin of untroubled Martin Cove and the more kinetic waters of Mahone Bay. Our first stop is the pebbled shoreline of Second Peninsula Picnic Park. Tables are set at the water's edge, which, unfortunately for baby strollers and wheel chairs, is down a steep embankment.

We're glad that the road sign predicts miles of twisty roads. It makes for good touring. We're almost to the end and are about to turn around when the water opens up on both sides of the road. Here a sandy isthmus joins the bony finger of Second Peninsula to the last island digit. On the right is a quiet inlet that seems like the subject of an old-fashioned mezzotint titled, "Pastoral Peace."

On the left is a completely different

picture. We park and follow a short path through the hardy grasses, silver artemesia, and trailing beach pea to a small tan-coloured beach. A generous surf is frothing up to a line of green-fleece seaweed (shaped like reindeer antlers). There are plenty of pebbles just asking to make a splash. We are captivated by half a dozen drumlin islands with high abrupt cliffs that trail away to gravel bars. Many more "ghost" islands lie just below the water's surface, the energetic tides. The sand we stand on may very well have been stolen from these ghosts.

LUNENBURG

DIRECTIONS

Leave Halifax on Route 103 west. Take Exit 10 at Oakland and follow Route 3 west through Mahone Bay to Lunenburg.

Leaving Yarmouth on Route 103 west take exit 11 at Blockhouse. Follow Route 324 south through Fauxburg and Northwest to Lunenburg.

The town of Lunenburg is an architectural wonder. Row upon row of century- and even centuries-old hand-crafted houses rest amongst mature shade trees in gradual steps down to the harbour. The commercial district, near the water is strikingly European looking too with its historic wooden structures. It remains a shopping and business area.

Lunenburg is the heart of Lunenburg County—the site where settlers first stepped ashore in 1753 and fanned out to populate the county and beyond. Public notices had been posted by the British government in Lunenburg, Germany, Switzerland, and Montbeliard. They advertised plots of land,

arms, and tools for housekeeping, land clear-
ing, house building, and fishing to suitable
applicants. The main criterion for suitability
was adherence to the Protestant faith. The
British government was looking to counterbal-
ance the numbers of French Catholic settlers
and native Mi'kmaq with a population that
would feel some loyalty to the British Crown.

In 1753 surveyors laid out a town in six
divisions of eight blocks. Each block was divi-
ded into fourteen town lots of 18.3 metres x
12.2 metres (60 feet x 40 feet). The settlers
may have been German-speaking but the **Lunenburg**

1. Fisheries Museum
2. Golf Course
3. Foundry
4. Tourist Bureau

Lunenburg Bay

street names were definitely British:
Cornwallis, Duke, King, Prince. Each settler
was allowed a town lot, a garden lot, a 121.5
hectare (300-acre) lot, and a 12.1 hectare (30-
acre) lot.

Lunenburg fared well even while settlements in other parts of Nova Scotia languished,
thanks to its rich farming soil and excellent fishing. Generations of wealth were built up
through offshore fishing and international trade.

With affluence, the houses became grander and more embellished. Simple dormer windows—originally added to bring sunlight into a dreary upstairs—became rooms unto themselves. Eventually they were designed to extend over the edge of the roof and connect to an extended entrance way to form a tower. There may have been some one-upmanship going on here, especially during the Victorian period. These roof protuberances have affectionately come to be known as "Lunenburg bumps." Some houses have bumps upon bumps upon bumps.

Lunenburg houses

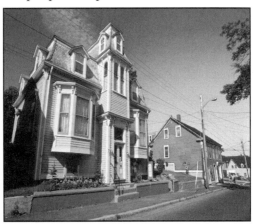

Recently the forty-eight block rectangle of the Old Town was designated a national historic district by the government of Canada. The town is an inspiration to anyone who appreciates architecture. Guided tours are available, or you can just take off on your own.

Little of the German language and culture is left in Lunenburg except for a slight drawl and a penchant for sauerkraut, Lunenburg sausage, and pudding (made locally with lots of summer savory). Family names have gradually become anglicized: *Wynacht* to "Whynot,"

Gorckum to "Corkum," *Mausser* to "Mouzar," *Klattenberger* to "Clattenburg," *Besancon* to "Bezanson," *Certier* to "Sarty," *Menegaux* to "Mingo," *Jolymoy* to "Jollimore," *Duvoisin* to "Davison." Lunenburg celebrates its annual Oktoberfest in late September and early October with a traditional German banquet, a biergarten, and other community events such as a pumpkin carving contest and a blessing of animals at St. John's Anglican Church.

SOUTH SHORE GENEALOGICAL SOCIETY

Many people are interested in their Lunenburg roots and the South Shore Genealogical Society (located on the third floor of the Fisheries Museum of the Atlantic) can help them. They have a collection of census records, cemetery inscriptions, church records, family genealogies, and many microfilms of other historical and genealogical interest. They charge a nominal fee to use their materials. The collection is constantly expanding as members donate their research to the society.

BLACK DUCK HANDCRAFTS CO-OPERATIVE AND GALLERY

The Black Duck Handcrafts Co-Operative and Gallery is an unusual gift and craft store with a lot of personality. It has been successfully run as a co-operative for twenty years and has done much to encourage cottage industries that produce traditional Lunenburg wares: witherod baskets, fishermen's woollen mittens (which used to be boiled into a felt-like texture), duck decoys, and birch brooms. A cornucopia of goods spills out of everywhere. Even the ceiling is peppered with wooden birds, birdhouses, and owner Marilyn McTaggart-Congdon's tropical fish, windsocks, and dragon kites. Years ago she started experimenting with scraps of colourful spinnaker sailcloth (rip-stop nylon) and now has quite a reputation as a performance-kite artist. Sometimes she attaches a number of windsocks to the line of a larger kite creating what she calls "kite laundry."

HOUSTON NORTH GALLERY

Houston North Gallery exhibits "the most talented and original self-taught artists from the Arctic and the Maritimes." It may seem incongruous to have northern art in Lunenburg, but very few of us will ever travel 2,000 miles north by bush plane to see Inuit art at its source. It is by necessity exhibited down south, so why not in Lunenburg? Owner Alma Houston lived on Baffin Island for years developing printmaking skills with the Inuit. She is credited with "awakening the world to Inuit art." Shows in the gallery include sculpture, prints, and tapestries.

LUNENBURG INDUSTRIAL FOUNDRY AND ENGINEERING LTD.

The hundred-year-old Lunenburg Industrial Foundry and Engineering Ltd. at 53 Falkland Street is a mainstay in this town. From the road we see an assembly of utilitarian red-brick factory buildings with small-paned windows. Less visible is a 137.2 metre (450-foot) wharf out back with three marine railways for hauling huge vessels up for repairs. Originally the foundry made cast iron stoves but in 1910 started producing the Atlantic Gasoline Engine designed by the plant's mechanical superintendent. The backbone of this business has been marine design, manufacture, refit, and repair for the fishing industry.

During the Second World War, the foundry refitted 104 ships for the Canadian navy as well as converting 8 whaling ships into minesweepers for the Norwegian navy. Today the company installs metal super-structures on wooden draggers and manufactures machinery for the scallop-fishing industry. Peeking in the window of the retail store we see an inventory of stoves, propellers, brass ships bells, and sundials. This substantial stuff is somehow a visual relief compared to the plastic fabrications we usually see at the mall.

LUNENBURG ACADEMY

The Lunenburg Academy is the towered fairy-tale castle everyone admires at the top of Gallows Hill, the highest point in town. It is an active school, as it has been since it opened its doors in 1895. Designed by a noted architect of the time, H. H. Mott from Saint John, New Brunswick, it cost $30,000 to build. The *Education Review* of February 1896 extolled a curious list of its virtues, including its "thoroughly modern style," the six entrances that afforded "a complete separation of boys and girls except in the classroom," a 272.8-kilogram (600-pound) bell (cast by Lunenburg Foundry), and speaking tubes connecting each floor with the basement.

Admiring the building from the outside, we are touched by this expression of the Victorian sensibility towards institutions for educating the young. They built it on the highest hill, with the best view around, with expansive windows to allow in lots of fresh air and sunshine. They also created a landmark that everyone could look up to with pride.

FISHERIES MUSEUM OF THE ATLANTIC

The Fisheries Museum of the Atlantic is the "genuine article." They sell authentic black Sou'Westers in the gift shop: lined and tarred with a wide slanted brim characteristically longer in the back to prevent sea water from going down the back of the neck—for only $29.95.

The touch tank invites us to "Touch only, please do not pick up." We pause and reflect. Do we really want to touch a starfish, a crab, a whelk, or a sea anemone? (Paper towels are provided.)

There's the ugliest fish contest between the sea pout and the sculpin. We think the sculpin wins hands down with its face that reminds us of an Agamemnon mask from Greek tragedy.

Dory Races at the Fisheries Museum of the Atlantic

There's a fish filleting demonstration (on video during the off hours) and the Solomon Gundy (pickled herring) taste test.

There are sheds chock full of boats, nets,

barrels, tools, sails, and "make-and-break" engines.

And there are real boats tied up to the wharf outside. We brace ourselves against the wind as we step aboard the creaky *Theresa E. Connor.*

Canada's 100th birthday in 1967 also marked the year the citizens of Lunenburg decided as a centennial project to refit an old ship called the *Theresa E. Connor.* She wasn't any old ship. She was a "twin-sparred saltbanker, long-hulled workhorse of the ocean, weathered veteran of thirty years of North Atlantic gales and rare survivor of the fleet that produced the world renowned schooner, *Bluenose.*"

This schooner that limped into Lunenburg Harbour in 1963 was the last of a dying breed of boats that fished the Grand Banks of Newfoundland by dropping tiny dories with men and their hand-lines into the dangerous swells.

Today the *Theresa E. Connor* is the heart of this museum dedicated to the fishing heritage of Atlantic Canada. In 1967 the good citizens of Lunenburg probably felt a great deal of nostalgia for the old ways of doing things. They took on the project with a spirit of optimism for the future and the new fishing technology. Today we feel doubly wistful for the days when there were so many fish that "120 long and lofty schooners so crowded Lunenburg Harbour that you could cross from shore to shore on their decks."

THE BLUENOSE

The *Bluenose,* born in Lunenburg, was an upscale elegant cousin of the *Theresa E.*

Connor. She was specially designed for a higher purpose—racing. In the 1920s the *Halifax Herald* established an international fishermen's competition, the Dennis Cup, to encourage improvements in the design of fishing vessels and the teamwork of their crews. After a season slogging it out on the Grand Banks, the *Bluenose* entered the race under the mastery of Captain Angus Walters and won. That was October 1921, and she won every year after that for eighteen years. In 1937 an image of the *Bluenose* was pressed onto the Canadian dime and has remained there, giving her icon status. She was a working boat but also the fastest in her class—and a beauty.

THE NOVA SCOTIA FISHERIES EXHIBITION AND FISHERMEN'S REUNION

The Nova Scotia Fisheries Exhibition and Fishermen's Reunion is a major community event. Captains, cooks, and crews of various fishing vessels host the Fishermen's Picnic "for 1,200 of their closest friends." For $6.00 guests are served a massive platter of haddock, halibut, and scallops, grilled on the spot. Other events include fish-filleting, scallop-shucking, and net-mending competitions.

THE TOURIST BUREAU

Even longtime residents of Lunenburg appreciate the climb up Blockhouse Hill Road to the Tourist Bureau—just for the view. We are overwhelmed by the extraordinary natural setting of the town. The Front and Back harbours are blue blue; the golf course is velvety green and rising on all sides—the wooded drumlin hills. Although a settler's perspective would have been different from our own, the blockhouse was built here in 1753 precisely because it commanded such an expansive view of the peninsula. Enemy ships sailing in the Front Harbour or hiding in the bays and inlets of the Back Harbour could be spotted long before they landed. If necessary, the settlers could retreat into the heavy timbered fortification and fight a defensive battle. The town also had a pentagon fort with another blockhouse and barracks (at the site of the Academy), and a tetragonal fort where the funeral home now stands.

BLUENOSE GOLF AND COUNTRY CLUB

The beautiful green park across the harbour from the Fisheries Museum is the Bluenose Golf and Country Club on Sheriffs Head. The steep nine-hole course on the side of a drumlin hill is a challenge. The very old hardwood trees along the harbour's edge complicate the course; seasoned golfers have been heard to say that they help stop balls from going into the drink. At one hole, golfers hit from on high and watch their ball drop 30.5 metres (100 feet) to the tiny green below, in the middle of an apple orchard. The course is so scenic that out-of-towners often pack cameras with their clubs.

LUNENBURG FOLK HARBOUR FESTIVAL

Every August Lunenburg is a Mecca for the folk-music faithful. The Lunenburg Folk Harbour Festival brings together performers who love their work and an audience who loves to hear it. The music is authentic and

Fiddlers at the Lunenburg Folk Harbour Festival

non-commercialized; the style is laid back. The mood permeates the town: for four days Lunenburg is bathed in music. Sea shanties float up the hill from the wharf stage; seagulls add a shrieking chorus. Music emanates from the bandstand in the town square, and at night the enthusiasm from inside the big tent spills out into the darkness. Hundreds of people crowd in to hear Appalachian tunes, traditional Scottish, Nova Scotian, and other "roots" music from entertainers such as Jeff Warner, Archie Fisher, Tom Lewis, Garnet Rogers, the Barra McNeils, and the Rankin Family.

LUNENBURG TO BLUE ROCKS

DIRECTIONS

Follow Lincoln Street east to Pelham Street. Continue east on Pelham Street and look for signs to "Battery Point, Blue Rocks, Garden Lots, Stonehurst." Continue east on Route 332 to Blue Rocks.

The harbour opens wide. On the other side of Lunenburg Bay, Ovens Point and overlapping Rose Point (near Kingsburg) drop sharply into the surf. From here that promontory looks like Blomidon. Our goal is Blue Rocks, the farthest point that we can reach by road on this side of the bay.

The view is superb but our eyes are fixed at ground level. We're checking the colour of the rocks. We see beige rocks, then grey rocks. There are fish sheds and century-old homes, and the road is very pretty. But there are no blue rocks in sight.

On the right we spot a sign to Herring Rock Road and we head down it. The houses here seem precariously perched—like those at Peggy's Cove or Prospect. And then—yes! The rocks are blue. Not so much Milk-of-Magnesia-bottle blue as muted slate-grey blue. This bluish slate is layered with quartz-grained sandstone and bent back on itself like so much massive ribbon candy. In geologic times huge thermal forces melted and heaved this rock into an undulating shape. The earth cooled and hardened in time for us to witness the result millions of years later.

At the end of the road a narrow planking atop a log cribbing leads down to a small wharf where boats offer whale- and bird-watching tours. Pamphlets describe what we might see: "Finback, pilot, humpback, minke whales, and porpoises, as well as ocean sun fish, sea turtles," and "reefs of seals soaking up the sun."

The nearby islands and ledges are a paradise for waterfowl and shorebirds: black ducks, common goldeneye, old squaw, scoter, and red-necked grebe.

PEARL ISLAND

We would especially like to see Pearl Island, one of the few offshore islands that still supports a diversity of seabirds (including Leach's storm-petrels, puffins, black guillemots, razorbills, common eiders, and terns).

Situated about 12 kilometres (16.6 miles) offshore, at the mouth of Mahone Bay, this small, treeless island is a designated wildlife area managed by the Nova Scotia Department of Natural Resources. Boats without an access permit must remain 800 metres (874.9 yards) offshore but boats with permits can come within 75 metres (82 yards).

Mather Byles DesBrisay in his *History of the County of Lunenburg* gives a humorous account of a trip in 1876 to Pearl Island (then called Green Island). He first had to sail from Chester to Tancook Island; the following morning he rowed 4.1 kilometres (3 miles) to Blandford, then on to Ironbound Island (where he feasted on a massive "plum-duff" prepared by the lighthouse keeper's wife). He then completed the largest leg of his voyage— alternately sailing and rowing to Green (Pearl) Island. The lighthouse keeper at that time was Albert Pearl after whom the island was later named. DesBrisay describes the noise and odour of the island—the nesting of countless "Mother Carey's Chickens" or "stormy petrel." He claims that the name petrel is derived from St. Peter because the birds, like Peter, had a "singular habit of running upon the water."

LUNENBURG TO RIVERPORT

DIRECTIONS

Leave Lunenburg south on Falkland Street.
Turn left on Tannery Road then right on
Masons Beach Road. At Masons Beach turn
left on Route 332 toward Bridgewater.

To get to The Ovens proceed through
Bayport and turn left on the Feltzen Road to
The Ovens Natural Park.

To get to Kingsburg and Hirtles Beach
continue on Route 322 to Rose Bay. Turn left
and follow the eastern shore of Rose Bay to
the end of the road.

Continuing on Route 332 through
Riverport you can return to Lunenburg on the
Indian Path or you may continue up the east
side of the LaHave River to Bridgewater and
Route 103. Or at East LaHave you can take
the ferry and travel up the west side of the
river to Bridgewater.

Heading down Falkland Street, just past
Lunenburg Foundry, we turn left on Tannery
Road and right on Masons Beach Road. At
Masons Beach we turn left on Route 332 to
Rose Bay.

We want to explore the southern side of
Lunenburg Bay right to its mouth (The Ovens,
across the bay from Blue Rocks). We travel
the scalloped edge of three great bays: Rose
Bay, Kings Bay, and Hartling Bay ending at
the sublime Hirtles Beach. We can double
back to Riverport and return to Lunenburg on
the Indian Path, or continue up to
Bridgewater and the Route 103, or cross on
the ferry to the west side of the LaHave River.

Tannery Road is the place to take a snapshot of the Lunenburg skyline. Travelling on

48

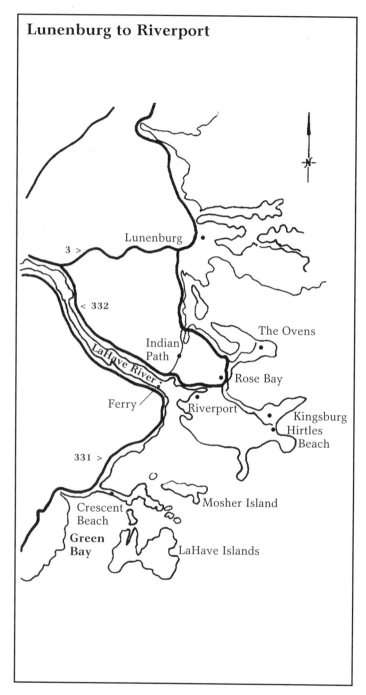

Lunenburg to Riverport

Lunenburg

3 >

< 332

The Ovens

LaHave River

Indian Path

Ferry

Rose Bay

Riverport

Kingsburg

Hirtles Beach

331 >

Mosher Island

Crescent Beach

Green Bay

LaHave Islands

to Puffeycup Cove (we love the name), we stop for a moment at a tiny beach to get our bearings. We can see the lighthouse at Battery Point, Cross Island on the horizon, and off to the right the rocky shoal at The Ovens. Just over the next drumlin is another spectacular lookoff—the causeway to Corkums Island. At Masons Beach we have the option of returning to Lunenburg (by turning right) but we turn left on Route 332. For the next 6.9 kilometres (5 miles) the road follows the sheltered back bays of Upper and Lower South Cove. At Bayport, plant guru Captain Dick Steele operates The Bayport Plant Farm specializing in rhododendrons, azaleas, heaths, and heathers. We promise ourselves to return in May or June when the rhododendrons and azaleas are in their glory.

THE OVENS

If we had come upon The Ovens without warning, stood at the top of the 30.5-metre (100-foot) cliffs and looked down, we would have thought that the world had turned upside down and probably that the gods were angry, too. Layers of slate laid down eons ago in an orderly horizontal fashion stand up sharply, on edge. The gouging surf has ravaged these cliffs, peeling them back layer by layer, and left huge caverns. We feel soft and expendable.

But we didn't come without warning. There's an entrance gate, a campground, a snack bar, and a swimming pool; and we've paid our admission and read a descriptive pamphlet before setting out on the trail with dozens of other people. There are well-maintained paths, secure handrails, and concrete steps with guarded fences built solidly into the rocks so people can walk down into the caves. There are all the signs that this place should not be intimidating to human beings.

But it is. We timidly venture down the steps into one cave (drip-dripping from the rocks above) in single file. And we step (jagged pieces of rock jutting out from walls and ceiling) inside the earth. At another chasm we stand tiny and cautious at the edge, as we wait for the next resounding BOOM of sea water pummeling the inside of some-where deep inside the cliff—somewhere dark that we have no desire to experience first hand. The Ovens is for "adventurers" who like the security of a handrail—and an ice-cream afterwards.

The village of Rose Bay has grown up on a half-mile-wide neck between Ritcey Cove (the LaHave River) and Rose Bay (the open Atlantic). This area is a microcosm of every-thing typically and dramatically Lunenburg County: heights of land overlooking beaches, spits, and reefs contrast with tidy cattle-cropped fields, and lovely homes. Every path offers a view of the water. There should be signs saying, "Caution: Drive Slow—Beauty Abounds." We find it hard to keep our eyes on the road. Oncoming cars have the same trouble and tend to slip over the solid line.

Kingsburg is a tiny village where time seems to have stopped in the nineteenth cen-tury. Planted onto the side of a hill the houses are close together but each one seems to be con-centrating on its own spot on the horizon. Be-yond the pond, the settler's burying ground, the protective rock wall, and the stretch of sand, is the vast blue where sky and sea merge.

The end of the road is Hirtles Beach. A photographer can offer visual images that speak for themselves. Describing the beauty in words is a difficult task. Our perspective is framed by the eroding gravel cliffs that cradle both ends of the beach. The waves are constant and demand our attention but our eyes are drawn to the watery horizon, which is punctuated by West Ironbound Island. We focus out to sea, to infinity.

On the outward side of the island a lighthouse marks the eastern side of Ships Channel, the major route for ships sailing up the LaHave River.

The western side of this channel is marked by a light on Mosher Island, the second largest island in the LaHave Islands group (best viewed from the Dublin Shore).

Without a boat, it's hard to get a sense of Riverport. The French came to the area in 1635 because it was situated just across the river from their fort, Sainte-Marie-de-Grâce. They cut down oak trees and fashioned them into planks, beams, and barrel staves for export to France. Later German and British settlers made a good living fishing, lumbering, and shipbuilding and built a lovely village at the edges of Ritcey and Creaser coves. In those days, going across to the other side of the river was like going across the street.

We drive all the way to the fish plants where a fleet of fishing boats often now lies idle. Beyond here are Five Houses and Oxners Beach, which back in time were of strategic importance. A cannon was kept here on watch and sounded to warn settlers inland if privateer sails appeared. The open flat sands were used for militia drill.

The Indian Path is believed to be just that. It is a creek bed that formed a natural path for ancient aboriginal peoples, early white settlers, and now for us. It is the shortest and easiest way to get from the LaHave River to Lunenburg Bay. A map dated 1744 by Jacques-Nicolas Bellin refers to it as Parks Creek, "the River where the portage is which goes to Mirligueche" (the Mi'kmaq name for the Lunenburg coast).

BRIDGEWATER

DIRECTIONS

Leave Halifax on Route 103 west. Take Exit 12 and turn left on North Street. Turn right on Aberdeen Road and continue across the bridge to King Street. Turn left at King to reach the town centre.

Leave Yarmouth on Route 103 east. Take Exit 14 at Hebbville and follow Route 3 east to the town centre.

Bridgewater

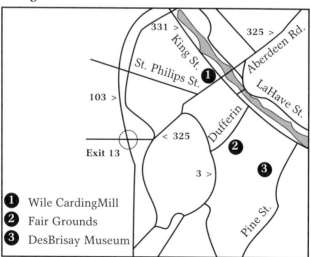

① Wile CardingMill
② Fair Grounds
③ DesBrisay Museum

BRIDGEWATER: MAIN STREET OF THE SOUTH SHORE

Bridgewater used to be all about the river but it's hard to know where the commercial heart of the town is now. Fire destroyed much of the wooden downtown core in 1899 and the old-fashioned businesses in the turn-of-the-century brick buildings have stiff competition from the malls, which are more convenient for drivers.

The downtown has a wonderful public library in a renovated bank building, an excellent family-run bookstore (Sagor's), a well-stocked health and gourmet food store (South Shore Natural Foods), and a couple of interesting men's clothing stores (Rofihe's is an institution). We love to peruse the special items at Cumings' Fire and Safety Equipment Ltd.: heavy-duty work pants, rubber fishermen's hats, fire extinguishers, and buoyant marine vests. It's also a good place if you're in the market for an instant fire escape or a safety vest. Every Sunday during the

Bridge over the LaHave River, Bridgewater

warm months a farmers' market mushrooms up overnight in the parking lot beside the river. They sell not only the usual produce such as corn and honey, but also driftwood art, European oysters, and heart-shaped waffles. Across the river is everyone's favourite hardware store, Gow's, which has kept its family touch even though it's expanded. Nails are still sold by the pound and rope off the spool. Our favourite time to shop there is Christmas, when the place is aglow and they cheerfully wrap our presents for us.

A mall with all the conveniences is just over the bridge on the eastern side of the LaHave River. It has the stores found in other malls all over North America, which reassures some travellers. Although it's situated on the lovely banks of the LaHave, for some reason it has no windows. There are two other malls in town. One has the liquor store; the other is home to the local movie theatre, the South Shore Cinema.

BRIDGEWATER TOWN PARK

There's a lovely greenspace in the middle of Bridgewater: 8.5 hectares (21 acres) of land that was donated to the town in 1921 by the Hon. W. H. Owen. The focal point of the town park is a large pond in a ravine-like setting. We enjoy feeding the ducks, who are quite spoiled. They are busybodies—diving for tidbits, nipping each other, and generally just steaming around the pond. They don't care to share with each other or the pigeons who also have to earn a living. Children enjoy the goldfish and the footpaths. They seem to need to run uphill, overtaking the more serious joggers and us plodding oldsters.

DESBRISAY MUSEUM NATIONAL EXHIBITION CENTRE

The DesBrisay Museum National Exhibition Centre is on the edge of the town park on Jubilee Road. This modern centre houses the oldest municipal collection of artifacts in the province. The history of the museum is one of the first exhibits on display. It tells the story of another age—that of the private collector.

In the 1870s Mather Byles DeBrisay collected just about everything, from a curious bird-shaped squash he picked up in Digby County (now very shrivelled) to a chunk of lava from Mount Vesuvius. This curious person, county judge, and historian established a private museum in his own home on Pleasant Street. In 1895 he wrote *History of the County of Lunenburg* after years of research. He describes his methodology in the preface to his book. Not only did he study the works of other writers and important public and private documents, he went out in the field.

"I have examined all the places of special historic interest referred to, and heard from the lips of many of the most aged residents, four of whom have attained respectively to ninety-five, ninety-six, ninety-eight, and over one hundred years, their personal recollections, and statements made to them by their ancestors." He managed to preserve for us the precious memories of people who were born 200 years ago.

DesBrisay's private collection eventually became a public one, and to honour his spirit, the museum was named after him. The exhibits contain a diversified collection of artifacts such as cannon shot from seventeenth-century muskets, to scale ship models, and a 6 1/2 horsepower make-and-break engine in mint condition manufactured by the now defunct Acadia Gas Engines Ltd. (a major employer in the area from 1907 to 1983). Travelling exhibits from other sources such as the Art Gallery of Nova Scotia and the Nova Scotia Museum enrich the permanent collection.

WILE CARDING MILL

Speeding down busy Victoria Road, we've seen the Wile Carding Mill dozens of times. A plain red shed, it sits on a quiet pond where lily pads float, maples bow, and a tiny brook babbles through. Lush grape vines twist their way up the side of the building and the steep creek bank. Inside the dimly lit structure is a collection of lumbering wooden and cast-iron machines. Puffs of wool dot the floor. "A cute quaint place this woolen mill," we think to ourselves.

Then our guide turns the hand crank to open the sluice gates. The water of Sandy Brook gushes through, the wooden wheel starts to spin, and we are thrilled to hear an entirely novel sound for modern ears—the thump, thump, thump of a water wheel going about the business of converting water energy into usable power.

And we can now imagine the thrashing and turning: how noisy those silent machines would be if they were attached to the shaft of that seven-horsepower water wheel. We notice how the walls and floor are black with the lanolin of sheep. And we can now imagine the heat and the smell of the place.

This mill shared the power of the brook with a dozen other industries over the years: a tannery, iron foundry, stone monument works, carriage factory, chair factory, grist mill, and sawmill. They lived cheek-by-jowl along the creek. The right to use the water was bought and sold, the flow controlled by dams. A sign next to the now peaceful pond states, "There were so many disputes that the area became known as Sebastapol after the long and bitter siege during the Crimean War."

And we think of Victoria Road as a busy thoroughfare *now*.

SOUTH SHORE EXHIBITION

Just what is an ox, anyway? Where does a cow leave off and an ox begin? What's the difference between a pulling horse and a draft pony? And what is the Strongman Competition and the Truck/Tractor Pull? All these questions and more are sure to be answered by going to the "Big Ex," (more formally known as the South Shore Exhibition) held every July.

Ox pull at the South Shore Exhibition, Bridgewater

The Ex is a traditional agricultural fair with a Lunenburg County twist. The well-trained oxen labour in tandem under red wooden yokes, and they're all gussied up in brass horn knobs, silver bells, and studded harnesses. Local Christmas-tree producers demonstrate wreath making. We enjoy wandering through the animal barns full of massive horses: Percherons, Heavy Belgians, and Clydesdales. There is usually some big-name entertainer on the stage but also lots of local talent: fiddlers, brass bands, arm wrestlers, horseshoe pitchers, and somersaulting gymnasts. The midway is always a big hit, too. We never miss an opportunity to test our nerves (and stomachs) on the ride we affectionately call "the barf bucket."

BRIDGEWATER LAHAVE RIVER FERRY LOOP

DIRECTIONS

Leave Halifax on Route 103 west. Take Exit 12 and turn left on North Street. Turn right on Aberdeen Road then left on LaHave Street. Follow LaHave Street to Route 3 through Dayspring. Turn right on Route 332 to Upper LaHave. Continue east on Route 332 to East LaHave. Cross the river on the ferry to LaHave. Turn right when you leave the ferry and follow Route 331 up the river and back to Bridgewater.

Leave Yarmouth on Route 103 east. Take Exit 13 and follow Route 3 turning right on Route 325 which becomes Victoria Road. Continue on 325 and Victoria Road to King Street. Turn right on King Street and leave Bridgewater on Route 331 through Pleasantville and West LaHave. Continue on Route 331 to the ferry at LaHave. Turn left when you leave the ferry and follow route 332 up the river and back to Bridgewater.

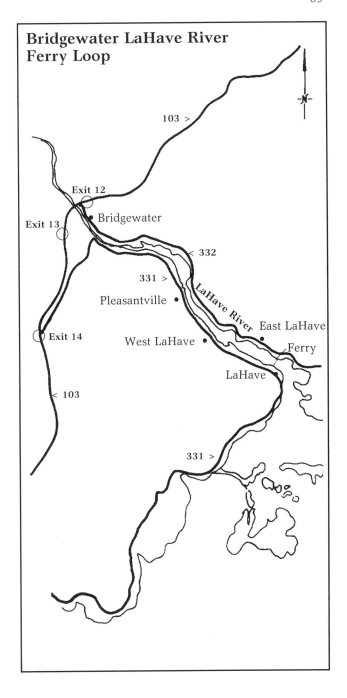

Bridgewater LaHave River Ferry Loop

103 >

Exit 12

Exit 13

Bridgewater

< 332

331 >

LaHave River

Pleasantville

East LaHave

Exit 14

West LaHave

Ferry

LaHave

< 103

331 >

After stopping off at the Apple Berry Farm Market across from the mall for some fudge and crisp Gravenstein apples, we set out for a drive down to the ferry, across and then up the LaHave River. It's an ideal lazy afternoon project. We're taking notes for an ongoing discussion about which side of the LaHave is more beautiful, east or west. We chase the river through the pine forest enjoying every curve and dip in the road. The river swells and goes through a personality change as it gets closer to the sea. This road was constructed before the invention of modern earth-moving machinery. It is a joy at 60 kilometres (37.2 miles) per hour. After that staying on the legal side of the road becomes a challenge.

THE LAHAVE FERRY

At fifty cents for the car and any number of passengers, a ride on the LaHave ferry may be the best transportation buy in the province. It is also a cure for doldrums of any sort, because no matter the weather, we get out on deck for the short passage across one of the most beautiful rivers in the province. Some call the LaHave the Rhine of Nova Scotia. The air is always fresh, the hills rise up magically around us and the ride is always too short. An underwater cable is the boat's lifeline, keeping it always on the same reliable path from shore to shore. In winter it's a curious sight to see the watery road the ferry cuts and recuts through solid ice, while close by hockey players weave around on skates.

In these automobile-dependent times, the view from the middle of a river is a rare treat. From the rail of the ferry we imagine this lush and tranquil river as it looked in 1632 when Isaac de Razilly first sailed in here. As lieutenant governor of New France he set up his capital and fort on the west side of the river, calling it Fort Sainte-Marie-de-Grâce. A museum now stands on the site.

LAHAVE BAKERY

The LaHave Bakery, a few doors down from the ferry, sells a fragrant mix of baked goods: heavy-seed bread, bagels, butter tarts, and our favourite gooey-on-the-inside dark chocolate brownies. Its unlikely location—on the banks of this lovely river, away from town—makes it a bit of a culinary miracle.

The bakery building with its warm wooden interior, curved glass display cases, and ornate pressed metal ceilings is worth visiting for its historic appeal alone. LaHave Outfitters used to supply provisions for the sailing ships that went out onto the Grand Banks for cod. The present owners also outfit boats, offering overnight berthing and anchorage for marine visitors.

BRIDGEWATER TO DUBLIN SHORE TO CHERRY HILL

DIRECTIONS

Leave Halifax on Route 103 west. Take Exit 12 and turn left on North Street. Turn right on Aberdeen Road then left on King Street. Leave Bridgewater on Route 331 through Pleasantville and West LaHave. Continue on Route 331 east through LaHave, and Dublin Shore.

To get to Green Bay, turn left after crossing the bridge at Petite Rivière. Continue east on Route 331 toward Broad Cove.

To get to Cherry Hill Beach, turn left at the fire station in Cherry Hill.

Continue west on Route 331 toward Voglers Cove and Route 103 at Mill Village.

Leave Yarmouth on Route 103 east. Take Exit 17 and turn right on Route 331 east to East Port Medway and Voglers Cove.

To get to Cherry Hill Beach, turn right at the fire station in Cherry Hill.

Continue east on Route 331 to Petite Rivière.

To get to Green Bay turn right before crossing the bridge.

Continue east on Route 331 through Crescent Beach, Dublin Shore, LaHave, and on to Bridgewater following the west side of the LaHave River.

Fort Point Museum is the site of a French fort built in 1632. Although the fort is gone and much of the point is now eroded, there's still a grand view of the LaHave Islands, especially Mosher Island, the second largest of the group. A lighthouse at its eastern tip is a beacon for boats heading through Ships Channel, the main passageway to the river. Ralph S. Johnson, in his book *Forests of Nova Scotia*, describes this island (formerly called Raspberry Island because of the profusion of berries): When the raspberries were ripe the island would be covered with passenger pigeons. They were a staple of the settlers of New France who killed them with sticks as they flew in flocks over the land.

At Dublin Shore we turn into Bells Cove for another look at the islands and the Felsen Kap across the river. The view from the end of the road is worth the trouble of having to double back.

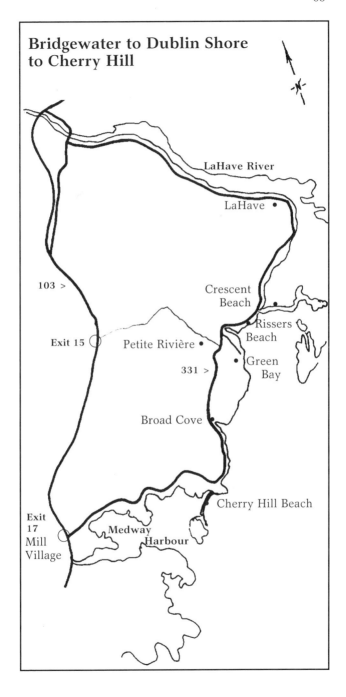

Bridgewater to Dublin Shore to Cherry Hill

LaHave River

LaHave •

103 >

Crescent Beach

Rissers Beach

Exit 15

Petite Rivière •

331 >

Green Bay

Broad Cove •

Cherry Hill Beach

Exit 17 Mill Village

Medway Harbour

CRESCENT BEACH AND
LAHAVE ISLANDS

A hundred years ago people drove horse and buggy across the sands of Crescent Beach to the islands. At low tide, several could travel abreast, leaving "but a faint impression." Unfortunately, today's trucks and all-terrain vehicles are much more obtrusive.

We drive behind the beach breakwater on a permanent asphalt road close to the gentler waters of Dublin Bay. This is a tombolo (the term for a sand bar that connects an island to the mainland). A luxurious stretch of sand fans out on our right as we zip through in the car. Clearly this beach would be better appreciated on foot.

On the islands old houses stand askew, on and beside house-sized boulders. They don't pretend to have anything to do with the modern road we've arrived on. A hundred years ago building a home on an island made perfect sense for fishermen. The most accessible place to dry fish was usually the best. The driveway was a wharf, the vehicle was a boat, and the highway was the water.

These islands were amongst the first in the New World to be seen and mapped. In 1604, even before finding Port Royal, De Monts and De Champlain gazed at the magnificent 30.5 metre (100-foot) bluffs of Cape LaHave (modern name). They baptized the island Cape de la Heve after the lighthouse at the entrance to their home port, Havre de Grâce, France.

Champlain's Cape is still uninhabited; the adventurous visit is made occasionally by boat or sea kayak to explore the hidden inlets, uninhabited beaches, slate

outcroppings, dunes, and woods of this outstanding archipelago.

The LaHave Islands Marine Museum,
which houses a collection of artifacts donated
by residents, is open in the summer and
staffed by volunteers.

RISSERS BEACH

Rissers Beach is a gorgeous crescent of sand,
perfect for swimming. We tune into the local
radio station (CKBW, 94.5 FM in
Bridgewater) for the "beach report," which
tells us the temperature of the water. We
pray for unseasonably high temperatures,
and no fog offshore. Rissers is usually recom-
mended. The water is the warmest on the
South Shore and the surf is predictable. We
patiently await every tenth wave—the big
swell worth diving into. Afterwards we soak
up the radiant warmth of the sand, until
we're hot enough to be tempted by the
waves again.

Rissers is a provincial campground with a
few seaside sites where lucky campers are
lulled to sleep by the lapping of the water.
Behind the beach a boardwalk has been built
across the salt marsh to give visitors a self-
guided tour of the fragile landscape.

PETITE RIVIÈRE

The town of Petite Rivière on the banks of the
feisty little river of the same name is probably
the most charming village on the South Shore.
Lovingly restored homes with well-tended
gardens face on to little lanes that thread the
wooded hills of the river valley. The iron
bridge is located at a busy corner. There's an
antique store, a second-hand clothing store,

and a boatbuilding shop. The old-fashioned large-paned store windows of Covey Island Boatworks are full of shackles and turnbuckles, marine charts, and brass objects. A few years ago, this shop built the *Tree of Life,* a wooden yacht that was named one of the "Hundred Greatest Sailing Yachts in North America" by *Sail Magazine* in 1993. Now they're involved in a project to build a new racing version of the *Bluenose* (to be called the *Bluenose Pride*) using their modern wood/epoxy laminating method.

GREEN BAY

Green Bay is a charming summer community a few miles down the road from Petite Rivière. Besides the obvious attraction of sand, waves, sunshine, and wild roses, people have been drawn here for generations by the promise of terrific pie and lobster chowder at the Canteen. The MacLeod family has been serving it here since 1929. Our favourite dessert is blueberry shortcake made with fresh wild berries, and a baking powder biscuit slathered with whipped cream. We always eat too much, and walk it off on the beach, padding in and out of the brisk surf until the daylight gives out.

Green Bay is also synonymous with "Mrs. Oickle's" (a.k.a. Ocean View Antiques), which has been in business for decades. Customers regularly travel from the city to look over the thousands of articles on display: everything from fine bone china, to leather horse collars, and primitive pine corner cupboards.

CHERRY HILL BEACH

Cherry Hill is *not* for the beach-ball set. For one thing, it's rarely hot enough here to wear a bikini. Even on the sultriest of days inland, a cold, clammy cloud of fog often stands in the wings.

But Cherry Hill is thrilling. It's a classic barrier beach—a sand spit so raw, wild, and unprotected it hardly qualifies to be called land at all. The line of sand is often littered with ocean throwup: headless seals and twisted mats of prehistoric-looking kelp. We love this beach because it challenges all our senses, with its raw iodine smell, ceaseless pounding breakers, and whipping wind. We are often too overwhelmed to open our eyes.

PORT MEDWAY TO LIVERPOOL

DIRECTIONS

Leave Halifax on Route 103 west. Turn left at Exit 17A at Mill Village and follow the signs to Port Medway.

From Yarmouth turn right at Exit 17A at Mill Village and follow the signs to Port Medway.

To get to Long Cove turn right on Harbourview Drive and follow the road along the shore of Medway Harbour to Medway Head and the end of the road.

Leaving Port Medway on the road to Mill Village, turn left at the intersection with the road to West Berlin. Turn right at West Berlin and follow the road through Eagle Head. Turn left on the Brooklyn Shore Road after crossing the bridge at Beach Meadows Brook.

To get to Beach Meadows Beach, continue 0.9 kilometres (0.6 miles) and turn left on the Beach Road.

To get to Brooklyn and Liverpool, continue east on the Brooklyn Shore Road to Route 3. Turn left on Route 3 to Liverpool.

PORT MEDWAY

Port Medway, population 285, sits at the very edge of Medway Harbour. As we drive from Halifax towards Yarmouth, this is the first in a series of beautiful but virtually unused harbours along our journey. Unused that is, compared to a century and a half ago, during the "Glorious Days of Sail" when the Maritime economy boomed. Half the pine exported from Nova Scotia went through Port Medway. Three thousand people lived here,

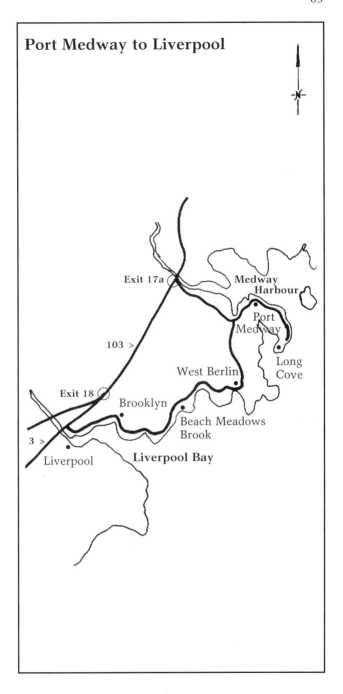

Port Medway to Liverpool

Exit 17a

Medway
Harbour

Port
Medway

103 >

West Berlin

Long
Cove

Exit 18

Brooklyn

Beach Meadows
Brook

3 >

Liverpool

Liverpool Bay

and the harbour was a forest of masts and billowy sails: barques, barkentines, brigs, brigantines, and schooners (many of them built right here).

Today the harbour is still prime for boating. There are some working fishing boats, but more small pleasure craft such as Boston whalers, sea kayaks, sail boats, and windsurfers. The mouth of the harbour is partially sealed by an archipelago of islands (Selig, Great, Middle, Toby, and Fryingpan islands), which fan out from Conrad (Cherry Hill) Beach. Seals frolic on the ledges and great blue herons, loons, and cormorants are common.

The Meeting House, on Long Cove Road, a provincial heritage property, was built in 1832 by the Freewill Baptist Open Communion Congregation of Port Medway. It is an architectural gem with simple roof lines, and a painted wood-panelled interior. The unusual pews built in the "Collegiate style" face one another in tiers rising to the high windows.

The Old Burying Grounds, behind Seeley's Hall on Queen Street, is situated on a magnificent bluff above the crashing waves of "Cemetery Beach" (where coffin handles and even human bones have been discovered). The inscriptions on the gravestones all face the road and are read as the visitor looks out to sea. Beyond them is a dramatic view out to the harbour mouth, Great Island, and the Long Cove Light. This graveyard is very old. The Proprietor's Records in the Registry of Deeds, Liverpool, contain the following entry: "Tuesday, March 28, 1786. Voted: that a Publick Burying Ground, containing one acre of land, be allowed and laid out at Port Medway."

Many old stones including the typical

skull with wings rising behind are in evidence. Many tell sad stories of men lost at sea and children dead before their time.

From one stone:

In memory of Captain Joseph J. Letson, who was lost at sea, October 13, 1874, aged 38 years old.

In Ocean Caves
Still Safe with Thee
The Germ of Immortality
and Calm and Peaceful is my Sleep
Rocked in the Cradle of the Deep.

PORT MEDWAY
TO LONG COVE

DIRECTIONS

Long Cove Road turns to gravel, but we persevere, following the harbour out to Medway Head, a barren of great boulders. Some compare this landscape to Peggy's Cove. Fire has scourged the land of trees, and with thin soil and lashing winds it will be a long time before they regenerate. But there is a stark beauty here and life, too: sphagnum moss, blueberries, juniper plants, rhodora, Labrador tea, and beach peas.

Standing high atop the rock cliffs we watch the turbulent waves rushing to meet the primordial greywacke rock. In August, after a Caribbean hurricane blows itself out on this shore, geyser-like columns of water rise up and explode like liquid fireworks.

At the end of the road we reach Long Cove, a finger inlet that has hosted a cluster of fishermen's sheds for many generations. During lobster season (as weather allows from November to May) the wharves are alive with activity. We park our car and are lured down the pebble road by the groaning foghorn and clanging bell buoy.

BEACH MEADOWS BEACH

Beach Meadows Beach, a ten minute drive from Liverpool, is a favourite of local people who walk the sands spring, summer, fall, and sometimes even winter. They tramp or jog from one end to the other and back—a measurable challenge. The cool sea air is always invigorating, and the sand underfoot is damp and firm. The gradually sloping sands produce dependably good surf. The best time of year for swimming is late August when the water is slightly less bone chilling.

Coffin Island (named after a person, not a casket) is the ever-present protector of the fragile sands of Beach Meadows. We see the light sentinel at the windward end. Fishermen have wisely built their wharves and stores at the other end.

The Municipality of Queens maintains a picnic park in the spruce thicket behind the dunes. Children delight in the freshwater pond behind the beach that is far more hospitable than the open sea. They try to catch the darting minnows. At the moist sand edge of the pond the footprints of children and gulls lead in and out of the water. We follow the stream as it wends through the soft sand to the open sea where it is invaded by salt water.

THE HANK SNOW PLAYGROUND FOR LITTLE CHILDREN, BROOKLYN

The Hank Snow Playground for Little Children in Brooklyn is a delightful place that's hard to miss. Huge "marshmallows" border the park: they're rocks painted not only in the traditional white, but also pastel shades of pink, blue, and green. Besides regular slides and swings, there are self-propelled rides: the roundabout, and four-seat spinning teeter-totter. The playground—on the site of the birthplace of Country and Western legend Hank Snow's birthplace—was built in 1979 by the Bowater Mersey Paper Company to celebrate its fiftieth anniversary.

HANK SNOW HOMETOWN MUSEUM AND COUNTRY MUSIC CENTRE

Hank Snow has founded an organization to help abused children. During his own difficult childhood he occasionally slept in the CN train station in Liverpool. The Friends of Hank Snow Society is building a museum and music centre on the station site at the intersection of Route 3 and Route 8. Plans include re-creating Hank's home office and recording studio at the Rainbow Ranch, Nashville, Tennessee, and displaying his 1947 Cadillac, amongst other memorabilia. It will also be home to Nova Scotia's Country Music Hall of Fame.

BOWATER MERSEY PAPER COMPANY LIMITED

Our first view of Liverpool Harbour includes the huge Bowater Mersey Paper Company Limited, which has been a major employer in Queens County since 1929. The original Mersey Paper Company was founded by Izaak Walton Killam, a financier from Yarmouth whose international holdings in publishing, utilities, construction, and films as well as pulp and paper, made him one of the richest

Canadians of his day and a great patron of the arts, education, and science. The current owner is Bowater Incorporated, an independent publicly traded corporation whose stock is traded in New York and London.

Occasionally tours are offered to the public. The mechanical, chemical, and electronic bowels of this huge plant are overwhelming. Here trees are debarked, chopped, cooked, mashed, and spread into massive paper-thin rolls. It is a state-of-the-art thermomechanical pulping plant that produces high-quality newsprint.

LIVERPOOL

Liverpool, Port of the Privateers—well why brag about it? Because these privateers were not really pirates in the strictest sense. Sure, they committed robbery on the high seas, but these were privately owned fishing schooners that had the blessing of the Royal government. It was a highly regulated business and **Liverpool** everyone made buckets of money, especially

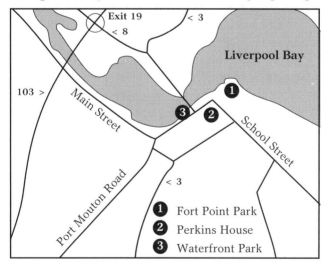

during the Napoleonic Wars when the Royal Navy placed embargoes on France and Spain. Privateers were also very important in protecting home ports such as Liverpool. Men much preferred joining a privateer ship commanded by a neighbour to being pressed into service by the Royal Navy. The Navy had the legal right to take anyone over the age of fourteen and in 1774 a frigate sailed into Liverpool Bay and did just that. It snatched thirty-five boys and men; we don't know how many of them returned.

During the American Revolution, the British government was grateful colonial

communities could help in disrupting the rebels' shipping lines. One ship, the *Liverpool Packet,* captured nearly 100 American ships and all the booty that went with it. Liverpool quickly became a busy prosperous port.

Fort Point, Liverpool

Looking for privateers we head down Main Street to Fort Point.

It's a nice park, with manicured lawns and trees planted in rows. We are happy to sit down at the bench next to the lighthouse and look out at the harbour as the sun goes down.

Bowater Mersey, the huge pulp and paper mill lights up across the way. The houses that edge the park are neat and tidy, and the asphalt abuts are trimmed in Kentucky Blue. As in any good neighbourhood, nothing is out of order.

If we were sitting here during the American Revolution, the scene would be much different. We would be watching for American ships that might sail into the harbour, in pursuit of our Liverpool vessels. We might see enemy sailors scrambling aboard our ships and cargo being tossed overboard. We would run for our lives as the Americans came ashore to loot our houses and wharves and to drag off our able-bodied men.

In 1780, American privateers entered Liverpool Harbour and captured Fort Lawrence, which used to stand on this point of land. A skirmish ensued, and Colonel Perkins with the militia immediately retook the fort. (We watched this exciting scene re-created here on placid Main Street during Privateers Day, a community festival held every July).

In 1763, 5 Riverside Drive was the site of Dexter's Tavern. The original house had just two rooms on the first floor—a common drinking room and a dining room. The upstairs had two bed chambers. Some say that the cut-stone foundation was brought from the ruins of Louisbourg.

Sixteen Main Street was built in 1767 by Captain Bartlett Bradford, a prosperous captain who fished off Labrador and St. Margaret's Bay and wintered in the Caribbean. After his sloop was seized in Port Medway Harbour and its cargo stolen, he took matters into his own hands and outfitted Liverpool's first privateer, the *Lucy.*

THOMAS RADDALL

Thomas Raddall, an award-winning author best known for his novel about Sable Island *The Nymph and the Lamp* and his popular history *Halifax, Warden of the North,* spent most of his adult life in Liverpool. In the quiet study of his home on Park Street he led a disciplined life and produced historical fiction that has done more to bring the past to life than many textbooks. His research was meticulous and thorough, and he was a great storyteller. His yarns often mesmerized listeners.

Raddall and a handful of others started the Queens County Historical Society, dedicated to collecting and preserving the human and natural history of Queens County. Their most extraordinary find was a yellowed manuscript, a diary written in spidery longhand by an early Liverpool settler—Simeon Perkins. Perkins faithfully kept the journal from 1766 until his death at age seventy-eight in 1812. It describes the everyday details of his domestic and business life. Raddall used this invaluable record as a prime source for a story called "At the Tide's Turn." Later, he expanded the theme of this story in his first historical novel, based on the early history of Liverpool.

SIMEON PERKINS HOUSE

Simeon Perkins was a native of Connecticut, one of many New England settlers who had moved to Liverpool between 1759 and 1765. When the American Revolution flared up these people were torn between family ties to the Thirteen Colonies and loyalty to the Crown. Their link with the Colonies was severed when Liverpool shipowners had to defend themselves against American privateers.

After discovering Perkin's diary, the Historical Society purchased the Simeon Perkins House on Main Street in 1936 and later deeded it to the Nova Scotia Museum. The restored home and museum next door are both open to the public. The Queens County Museum at 109 Main Street maintains extensive archives: early deeds, land grants, marine documents, business journals, more than 3,000 photographs, and other records of interest to genealogists. The archives have been named The Thomas Raddall Research Centre.

Simeon Perkins House and the Queens County Museum

THE LIVERPOOL WATERFRONT PARK

The breeze off the Mersey River makes the waterfront park a cool relief on a hot summer day. This strip of grass—between the Mersey River and Main Street (just off the bridge on Bristol Avenue)—offers a wide view of the river's mouth. The tourist bureau is here, as well as a children's playground and a farmers' market. The stores are just up the hill. This is the charm of Liverpool—small enough for residents to walk to the post office, library, bank, hardware, and grocery store. After Sunday church services the streets are filled with families dressed up walking home together.

ASTOR THEATRE

Known as the Opera House and built in 1902 as an adjunct of the old Town Hall, the Astor Theatre is still a going concern. It is one of the few old stages that has continually supported live performances throughout the entertainment revolution of film and television. A volunteer society runs the theatre and there's a special feeling in attending performances here. It's a community gathering spot. Friends take tickets and give out programmes. The Astor, over the years, has hosted such talents including Rita McNeil, Mr. Dressup, Liona Boyd, the Royal London Shakespeare Company, and as many community groups. The international Amateur Theatre Festival has been held here. An extremely active community theatre group, the Winds of Change, performs here several times a year. On weekends, films (ranging from the commercial to classics) are shown.

LIVERPOOL TO MILTON-MERSEY RIVER LOOP

DIRECTIONS

Leave Halifax on Route 103 west. Take Exit 19 and turn left on Route 8 south to Liverpool.

From Yarmouth, take Route 103 east to Exit 19 and turn right on Route 8 to Liverpool. Turn right on Bristol Avenue. Continue east on Bristol Avenue and Market Street to Main Street. Turn right on Main Street and follow the Milton Road north, up the east side of the Mersey River. Cross the Mersey River on the second bridge at Potanock Street. Turn right on Route 8. Follow Route 8 south through Milton and back to Route 103.

Starting at the town hall in downtown Liverpool, we travel north with the river on our right towards Milton West. At the second bridge, we turn right to cross the Mersey River on Potanock Street, and right again on Route 8 travelling south, with the river on our right, back to Liverpool

Drive, pedal, or better still, walk this loop along both sides of the Mersey River through the small village of Milton. It's an old-fashioned country road—with mature chestnut and locust trees, comfortable old homes, and a river that perfectly mirrors the sky.

SYLVANUS COBB

Our first good view of the river is at a tiny park at the corner of Main Street and Wolfe Street. Children spin on the roundabout while their parents inspect the historic cairn. It's dedicated to Captain Sylvanus Cobb, "Patriot, Soldier, Sailor, and Pioneer, 1709–1762," who served at the first and second sieges of Louisbourg and with Wolfe at the capture of Quebec. He was one of the first settlers of Liverpool in 1759 and built a frame house on this spot on the riverbank.

TUPPER PARK

Tupper Park is at the foot of the first bridge. We relax at a picnic table, lulled by the sound of rushing water. Four mills once harnessed the power of the current here. They were a great maw for logs boomed upstream, transforming them into millions of board feet. All that remains now is the dam and a fish ladder to help Atlantic salmon get upstream to spawn. Occasionally the fish hatchery restocks the river by piping a truckload of small wriggling salmon or trout off the bridge here. What a joyful sight!

There are two rocks in Tupper Park with plaques embedded in them. The first is dedicated to Margaret Marshall Saunders who was born in Milton in 1861. She wrote twenty-five books but her most popular was *Beautiful Joe*, the autobiography of a dog who is rescued from his brutal owners. Saunders entered it in a literary contest held by the American Humane Education Society and won. It became the first Canadian book to sell more than a million copies and was published in fourteen languages. A passionate defender of animal welfare, the author donated most of her royalties to humane societies.

Another plaque is dedicated to the memory of wood sculptor Ralph Boutilier, "Dean of Nova Scotia Folk Artists, 1906–1989." Born in Boutiliers Point, Halifax County, he lived much of his life here in Milton. A self-taught painter, he didn't start carving in wood until 1968 when he was sixty-two years old. He created kinetic sculptures: birds with wings that flapped. He made his own tools, fashioning a lathe out of an old washing machine. Many of his pieces are owned by private collectors, but his life-size wood carving of Simeon Perkins watches over the famous diary at the Queens County Museum on Main Street in Liverpool.

THE MILTON BLACKSMITH MUSEUM

The Milton Blacksmith Museum sits across from the park. A largely volunteer effort by the community has brought more than 22,000 artifacts together in a fascinating collection. There's a warm ambiance to this naturally lit building. At its heart is a floor-to-ceiling forge where metal is still occasionally melted to red-hot and pounded into a grub hoe, a wagon part, or shoes for an ox. The prize of the collection has got to be the ox sling. Hand-hewn timbers and canvas, chains and rings are part of this contraption. In its day it hoisted the huge beasts off the ground so that they could have iron shoes nailed onto their unusual split hooves (each shoe has two pieces).

The Milton Blacksmith Museum, Milton

The museum has a photography collection of Milton homes from the mid-1800s when lumbermen were kings. We look for these homes as we journey up the river, cross the second bridge (where rubble remnants of more mills can be seen) and head back to Liverpool on the opposite bank. The Milton Heritage Society has done an inventory of the domestic architecture of the area. Both sides of the river (on Main Street and West Street) have Cape Cod style homes predating 1850. They have documented nineteen Gothic Revival houses with the typical central dormer and gothic window. What we find most interesting about these homes is that they were almost entirely built out of local materials by local artisans. The barge boards, mouldings, brackets, and windows were all manufactured beside this river out of trees cut close by. That says a lot about the self sufficiency of the times.

PINE GROVE PARK

At the end of the Milton loop and within a stone's throw of the big highway (Route 103) is Pine Grove Park. Here on the banks of the Mersey River, 21.9 hectares (54 acres) of cathedral-high, 130-year-old white pines have been preserved by the Bowater Mersey Paper Company. Walking amongst these giants we get some sense of what the first Europeans saw when they came here 200 years ago. Mature stands of trees like these once covered the banks of all the great South Shore rivers—the Mersey, the Medway, and the LaHave. Soon, the mad scramble to feed Europe's appetite for wood created a shipbuilding industry. Boats were built to carry the wood to Europe, and the forests were decimated.

These woods are cool and fragrant. The forest floor is cushioned with pine needles and cones worthy of any child's collection.

Bowater's staff has not only worked hard to preserve this forest, but had done much to diversify and enhance it. The dead lower limbs have been trimmed and sheltered beneath the trees are over 600 varieties of rhododendrons, azaleas, heathers, and heaths. Curiously, these exotic cousins—plants from the Himalayas, Japan, and the Carolinas—thrive in the shady, acidic environment of native pine. The world is much smaller now than it was 200 years ago.

The park is a balm for weary travellers. Reaching the gravel bank of the river we cool our toes and skim a few pebbles across the surface of the Mersey.

LIVERPOOL TO WESTERN HEAD LOOP

DIRECTIONS

Leave Halifax on Route 103 west. Take Exit 19 and turn left on Route 8 south to Liverpool. Or from Yarmouth, take Route 103 east to Exit 19 and turn right on Route 8 to Liverpool. Turn right on Bristol Avenue. Continue east on Bristol Avenue and Market Street to Main Street. Turn left on Main Street and proceed two blocks south to School Street. Turn right on School Street and proceed east past the hospital to the Western Head Road. Keep to the right and follow the road to Western Head, Mersey Point and back to School Street.

From downtown Liverpool take Main Street towards Fort Point. Turn right on School Street and drive past Queens General Hospital to the sign to Mersey Point/ Western Head. At the fork stay on the right towards Western Head.

Liverpool is situated at the mouth of the Mersey River where it feeds into Liverpool Bay. This bay is pretty, thank you, but when

Liverpudlians crave the real ocean they head
out to Western Head. On a stifling hot summer evening the moist fog hanging over the
point is a heavenly relief. After a winter
storm the raging fountains of salt spray are
amazing to witness.

It's a 4-kilometre (2.5 mile) drive inland
before we reach the shore. The ocean view
breaks through at Victoria Lake where the
fresh water is protected from the salty waves
by a barricade of beach rocks. Every rock
here has been pummeled into roundness.
With each swell they are scooped up and
hurled up the embankment. They roll back
down only to be scooped up again and again.

We turn left and drive a ledge secured by
the same rubble embankment. A mile down
the road is the turnoff to the Western Head
Light. (Not a lighthouse, because like so many
other lights, it is unmanned. The house is
boarded up.)

On a clear day we see for miles, up to the
next light on Coffin Island and beyond. The
shore is all greywacke bedrock and loose
rough rocks, not great for walking distances.
But we are content to just sit and observe the
subtle coloration—the blue greys, green greys,
tan greys, and the reflected light and shadow.

Returning to town we enjoy the pan-
orama down over the cozy cove at Moose
Harbour. Boats are tied up at the wharf.
Liverpool Bay is on the horizon.

SAVAGE GALLERY

Savage Gallery features the artwork of Roger
Savage. He specializes in watercolours
painted outdoors on location. We notice that
the artist has captured the subtle tones and

forms of the rocks we have just surveyed at Western Head. Particularly striking are his paintings and prints of Cadden Bay (the Kejimkujik Adjunct).The gallery is a bright cheerful space. The walls are covered with dynamic and colourful paintings, but we can't help staring out the back windows at an exquisite clump of honeysuckle and our continuing perspective of the Bay out to Coffin Island.

WHITE POINT TO SOUTH WEST PORT MOUTON

DIRECTIONS
Leave Liverpool on Route 3 west. Turn left at White Point to get to White Point Beach.

Continue west on Route 3 through Hunts Point and Summerville Beach. At Summerville turn left on Route 103 and proceed west to Port Mouton.

To get to Carter's Beach, turn left in Port Mouton and follow the signs through Central Port Mouton toward South West Port Mouton. Turn left on the Carter's Beach Road and park at the end of the road. The beach is a short walk along the path at the end of the road.

To get to the Kejimkujik National Park Seaside Adjunct continue west on Route 103 from Port Mouton. Turn left on St. Catherines River Road at Robertsons Lake and the head of Port Joli. Follow St. Catherines River Road for approximately 6 kilometres (4 miles) to a large parking area on the left. The beach is a forty minute walk along a well marked trail.

This road faithfully follows the shoreline of Port Mouton, a pocket-shaped, sand-lined harbour. Along its shore are tiny resorts and

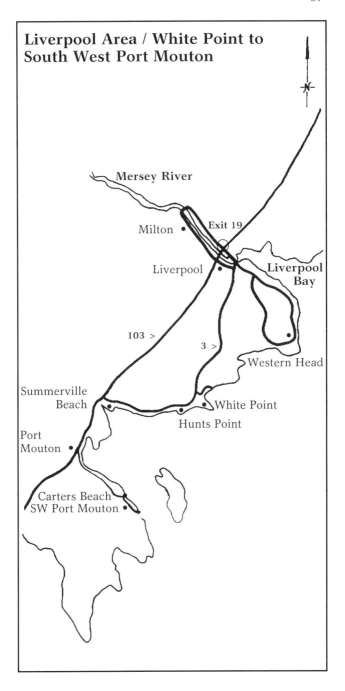

Liverpool Area / White Point to South West Port Mouton

Mersey River

Milton

Exit 19

Liverpool

Liverpool Bay

103 >

3 >

Western Head

Summerville Beach

White Point

Hunts Point

Port Mouton

Carters Beach
SW Port Mouton

lovely beaches at White Point, Hunts Point, Summerville, Port Mouton, and South West Port Mouton.

Most visitors get to White Point Beach—a spectacular barrier beach—and the lake behind it called Doggett's Pond through White Point Beach Lodge. The lodge offers day passes to people not staying the night that allow use of the indoor swimming pool. On a cold, distinctly unbeach-like day we prefer to watch the roaring surf through the glass at pool side. Local residents and the public in general have deeded access to the beach on a path that crosses the second and sixth fairways of the golf course.

THE LIVERPOOL GOLF CLUB

The Liverpool Golf Club at White Point is for nature lovers. Three or more holes border the ocean. Hole six is immediately next to the surging whitecaps. All manner of migrating seabirds, geese, and ducks continually fly over the course. Some local golfers arrive very early in the morning to greet the deer who become a bit ball-shy later in the day. The course is open to the public and all equipment can be rented, including motorized carts.

Hunts Point Beach is right at the road's edge. To get off the highway we take a short road that leads to the government wharf. We like to climb on the huge boulders at the end of the beach, to watch the fishing boats and beach activity from a vantage point. It's a perfect perch for a sketching artist.

Summerville Beach, a wide swath of sand wedged between salt water, salt marsh, and the Broad River, has been a favourite swimming and sand-castle beach for generations (with fish and chips and ice-cream close by). This provincial park is also a protected beach. Boardwalks shield the dunes and marram grass from trampling feet that create erosion blowouts. When piping plovers are nesting, sections of the beach and parking lot may be cordoned off to visitors.

We stop by Mersey Point Fish at 335 Central Port Mouton Road hoping that the doors of the smokehouse will be open so that we can get a glimpse of the fillets hanging from hooks above the smouldering, aromatic maple fire.

The Mutsaers family emigrated to Nova Scotia from Holland a decade ago bringing with them cherished recipes for smoking and pickling salmon, mackerel, eels, and herring. Their smoked salmon *Nova* is more delicate and less salty than other varieties.

CARTERS BEACH

It is amazing that although there are literally hundreds of beaches along the South Shore of Nova Scotia, each one has its own personality. What sets apart Carters Beach (and, continuing up the shore, Wobamkek Beach) are their massive sand dunes—heaps of snow-white powdery crystals piled fifty feet high. On a sunny day the banks glisten from across the harbour. We imagine that they were a welcoming flag to the French as they explored this coast in the early seventeenth century. There were no wharves, breakwaters, lighthouses, or even village fires to distinguish one bay from the next. What sailors looked for was a friendly flat plane on which to land a boat without being smashed on the rocks. A sand beach was perfect.

In 1604 Pierre Du Gua de Monts, on an expedition to colonize Acadia and short of supplies, stopped over on this beach with the huge sand dunes. One hundred and twenty soldiers, craftsmen, and priests came ashore. In the process, a sheep fell overboard, and the newly discovered harbour was christened Port au Mouton.

They stayed long enough to build huts for shelter. They performed a religious service on the beach (believed to be the first Christian service in North America) and Samuel de Champlain sketched a map of the area illustrating it with moose and rabbits.

Carters Beach is indeed a blessed spot. The pure white sand is embellished with shell medallions of sun-bleached sand dollars. Beneath the tide are thousands of their living counterparts: fascinating creatures, velvet to the touch.

PORT L'HEBERT POCKET WILDERNESS

After a long drive, we appreciate a scenic walk that begins right off the main road. The 3-kilometre (1.9 mile) walking trail in the Bowater Mersey Port L'Hebert Pocket Wilderness Area leads to the head of Port L'Hebert Harbour (named after Louis L'Hebert, Champlain's apothecary, in 1604). It's described as typical South Shore land— burned over many times, but regrowing aspen and birch now sprout up amongst huge lichen-splashed granite boulders. Our walk through the young and fragile forest culminates with a magnificent view of the harbour and vast salt marshes—a wildlife sanctuary. We are told to look for bald eagles and warblers, toads, and snakes. This area is well-known as a wintering ground for migrating Canada geese. Eel grass, open water, and minimal disturbance allow them to survive the harsh winter months here.

The natural and cultural history of the Port Joli area is celebrated each July at *Discovery Days* . Sponsored by the Port Joli Basin Conservation Society (a non-profit organization dedicated to protection of the area between the Kedge Seaside Adjunct and the Raddall Provincial Park), activities include naturalist-guided tours, sea kayaking, bird walks, and lectures on native plants.

KEJIMKUJIK NATIONAL PARK SEASIDE ADJUNCT

In Nova Scotia there are many beaches we can drive right up to and some—like the Crescent Beaches to Lockeport and on the LaHave Islands—we can even drive *on.* But there is one beach that must be approached respectfully, on foot: the Kejimkujik National Park Seaside Adjunct (a.k.a. Cadden Bay, St. Catherines River Beach, and the Woods Property).

This magical place is one of the last untouched stretches of sand along the South Shore: 4.1 kilometres (3 miles) of beach where the insults and injuries of all-terrain vehicles, motor boats, and shotgun blasts will never be felt. Piping plover, white-tailed deer, and harbour seals have dominion here. It is a national treasure and the federal government is committed to protecting the 22 square kilometres (8.5 square miles) of beaches, coves and lagoons, rocks, tidal flats, and pristine white sand—and the plants and animals that live here, too.

Two footpaths into the park come out at

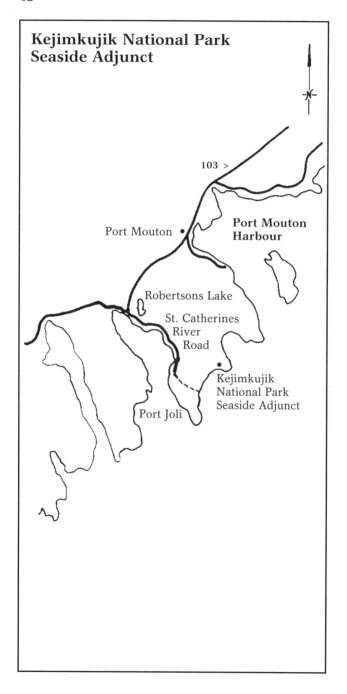

Kejimkujik National Park Seaside Adjunct

-N-

103 >

Port Mouton

Port Mouton Harbour

Robertsons Lake

St. Catherines River Road

Kejimkujik National Park Seaside Adjunct

Port Joli

opposite ends of the beach: a 3-kilometre (1.86-mile) walk on a cart track from St. Catherines River and an 8-kilometre (5-mile) walk on an old gravel road from South West Port Mouton. The park brochure describes them as "rough and wet" and recommends sturdy waterproof footwear. A boardwalk gives access through the wetter areas. The longer route is open to mountain bikes, but ends at a tidal sluice that is sometimes very swollen and passable only by boat or by swimming across.

We opt for the shorter walk across the cranberry bog. It's a cool fall day and the berries are red and ripe. They "pop" delightfully between our teeth, but are desperately sour. We rub a Labrador tea leaf between our fingers to confirm that it's bog perfume is what permeates the air. Almost before we know it we've arrived. We hear the roar before we see the beach. No matter that we've been here before: the first glimpse from on high of this huge expanse leaves us speechless. We sit on a sun-warmed rock to have lunch in paradise. Why does food always taste so much better outside?

SHELBURNE COUNTY

CASTAWAY IN SHELBURNE COUNTY

No, we don't want to be "cast away," as in thrown away and abandoned for all time. What we *do* want is to get the feeling, occasionally, of being a solitary person in a deserted place. We need to feel like a minute speck in the universe—to regain a sense of awe. This happens when we are alone with the breakers and the rocks and the wind that whips in and out of our ears.

Shelburne County is a castaway kind of place. Scanning topographic maps we search for secluded shoreline. Many areas are totally inaccessible by road. We wonder how these places ever got named. They've barely been visited by humans. There are dozens of beaches that can be reached only by hiking down old woods roads or on gravel roads (faint lines on our map). We like to ask directions at the local store or service station. Whenever we get a chance, we explore castaway places, but with preparation and caution.

Roads into uninhabited places may be far from scenic. It's not uncommon to drive for an hour through alder scrub and cheek-by-jowl human habitation to find heaven at the end of the road. Such trips shouldn't be attempted before the summer road grading season. (Heavy spring rains often wash roads out.) Before setting out we check our fuel and tires (and the spare) and pack food, gum boots, a flashlight, and extra outerwear.

Detailed maps are essential. The 1:50,000 topographic map series published by the Federal Department of Energy, Mines and Resources is excellent. Symbols differentiate between a sandy and a rocky shore and show outstanding bluffs and offshore rocks. Little

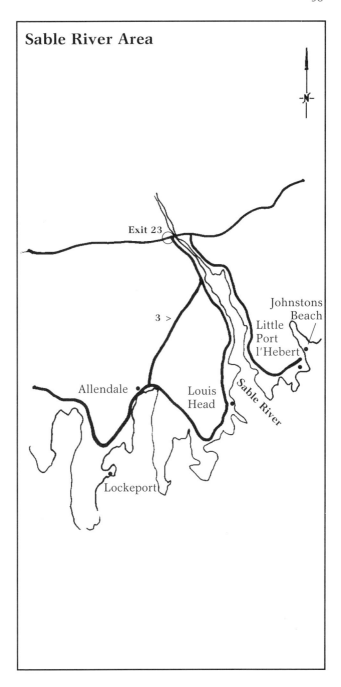

Sable River Area

Exit 23

3 >

Johnstons Beach

Little Port l'Hebert

Allendale

Louis Head

Sable River

Lockeport

black squares mean buildings. Often we can predict how good the view will be by measuring the distance from the road to the shore.

LITTLE PORT L'HEBERT

One out-of-the-way place is the tip of the peninsula between the Sable River and Port l'Hebert. Leaving Route 103 we take a road behind the Grug and Grog Restaurant. It almost immediately turns to gravel and for half an hour there's little view of the water. The farther we travel the narrower the road becomes. The shoulders disappear and the bush on both sides has been hacked back just enough to not rip the mirrors off the car. We have to carefully negotiate deep ruts and muffler-grazing outcroppings.

We begin to question our undertaking— and then we arrive at the rock rampart behind Johnstons Beach. Here are the most tempestuous green frothy heaving breakers we've yet discovered along this shore. On the inland side of the rock barrier are the vast clam flats of Johnstons Pond.

There are miles of shoreline to explore here. A path along the cliff edge threads back to a tiny harbour called Little Port l'Hebert. Much of this headland (known as Richardson Head) is privately owned; the owners do tolerate visitors who respect the landscape but assume no responsibility for use (turn left at the sign to Little Port l'Hebert Properties). Although this is just the end of a peninsula, we feel as though we're at the wild ends of the earth.

Travellers need time, patience, and common sense to explore castaway places. Some other remote destinations are: Round Bay/ Atlantic, Ingomar, Blanche, and Baccaro.

LOCKEPORT AND AREA

DIRECTIONS:

Leave Halifax on Route 103 west. Take Exit
23 at Sable River and follow Route 3 west
through Allendale to Lydgate. Turn left at
Lydgate and follow the Brighton Road to
Lockeport.

To get to the Sable River Picnic Park follow Route 3 west about .5 kilometres (.3
miles) from Exit 23.

To get to Louis Head continue another 3
kilometres (2 miles) on Route 3 west. Turn
left at West Sable and follow the West Sable
Road along the shore of Sable River to the
ocean. Look for signs for Louis Head Beach
and the Louis Head Breakwater Road.

Leave Yarmouth on Route 103 east. Take
Exit 24 at Jordan Falls and follow Route 3 east
through East Jordan to Lydgate. Keep right at
Lydgate and follow the Brighton road to
Lockeport.

To get to Louis Head continue east on
Route 3. At Allendale turn right on the Little
Harbour Road. At Little Harbour turn left on
the West Sable Road. Look for signs for Louis
Head Beach and the Louis Head Breakwater
Road.

To get to Sable River Picnic Park continue north on the West Sable Road. Turn
right at Route 3 and proceed about 3
kilometres (2 miles) east to the park.

SABLE RIVER PICNIC PARK

The Sable River Picnic Park is a tiny sanctuary of green along Route 103 from Halifax to
Yarmouth. It's a good place to cool off and
decompress after being trapped in the metal

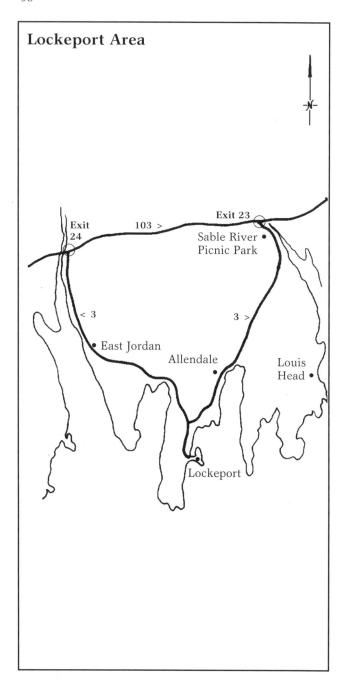

Lockeport Area

Exit 24

103 >

Exit 23

Sable River
Picnic Park

< 3

3 >

East Jordan

Allendale

Louis
Head

Lockeport

box of a car on a hot summer's day. We wash our hands under a gushing hand pump and stay awhile listening to the crickets.

LOUIS HEAD

Louis Head Beach, about ten minutes from Route 103 on Bills Cove, is a good swimming beach. Because the Sable River is shallow here, the waves are warmish and roll in at a regular clip. More-or-less permanently planted trailers are parked behind the sand.

Our favourite spot is just down the road—the Louis Head Breakwater, which has three distinct personalities. One side is a shallow sheltered cove. The end of the road is the breakwater—a manmade rock barrier that penetrates the harbour, disrupting the natural patterns of ocean, moon, and gravity. The waves splash vertically in a sequence like a line of fire. The effect if hypnotic. The light is intense: the golden rod and purple aster are particularly vibrant with a threat of frost in the air.

For a third point of view we climb over the wall of beach rocks. We are awestruck by the sight of the outer harbour: the gravel hill of Raspberry Head and the massive rollers coming straight at us.

LOCKEPORT

"Lockeport," wrote Clara Dennis in 1934 (author of *Down in Nova Scotia),* is "the quaintest little town in all Nova Scotia." Although this community has had some tough times since the downturn in the fishery, we have to agree. There's something special about a town that lives its life within the confines of an island. Every house has elbow room but that's it. Every street ends with a fresh blue view. No getting lost in Lockeport.

The town is tethered to the mainland by beautiful Crescent Beach, and a road along the back of the beach gives automobile access. Crescent Beach is picture-perfect but civilized. (It used to grace the back of the Canadian fifty-dollar bill.) There are new modern change houses, fresh-water showers, and flush toilets.

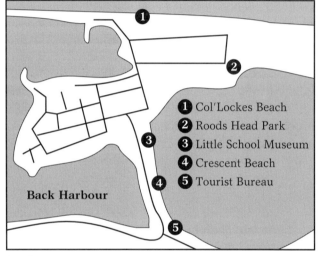

1. Col' Lockes Beach
2. Roods Head Park
3. Little School Museum
4. Crescent Beach
5. Tourist Bureau

Back Harbour

Lockeport   Lockes Island was named after one of the first families to settle here. Jonathan Locke, M.D. was amongst the handful of pre-Loyalists who arrived circa 1760. The family settled in a cozy cove, where they built wharves. The flourishing West Indies trade and limitless amounts of fish made them wealthy. Between 1836 and 1876 the Lockes built five dwellings next door to each other. These Colonial, Georgian, and Victorian homes are all still standing. In 1988, the Locke Family Streetscape on South Street became the first provincially registered streetscape in Nova Scotia. Much of Nova Scotia must have felt like this place at one time—elegant well-built homes with sand beaches and working wharves almost at their doorsteps. That was when the boat was the vital transportation link with the outside world and a living was made at sea.

Rood Head Point is a bit of wilderness on the southeast corner of this otherwise settled island. We scale the wooded cliff and then the fog, like so much smoke, pours over us. We can hear the waves breaking all round, but cannot see a thing. Then the sun breaks through, burning an opening to the rocks below. We can see enough to know how precariously we are perched.

SHELBURNE

DIRECTIONS:

Leave Halifax on Route 103 west. Take Exit 25 and follow Route 3 west to Shelburne.

Leave Yarmouth on Route 103 east. Take Exit 27 at Birchtown and take Route 3 east to Shelburne.

Shelburne is everyone's idea of a relaxed small town: a generously wide tree-shaded main street, old-fashioned storefronts displaying dry goods behind expansive windows, and lots of parking space, some on the diagonal. The mini-mall, on the way into town is busy, but Water Street is still the main drag, where people smile and say hello even if you're "from away."

SHELBURNE: A LOYALIST TOWN

The Dock Street district—between Water Street and the harbour—is the Loyalist heart

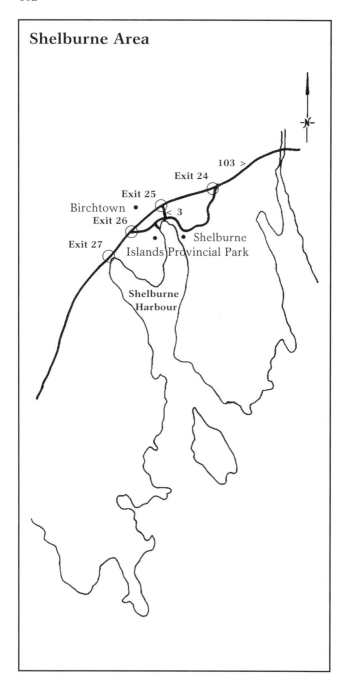

of Shelburne. Dozens of eighteenth-century buildings have miraculously survived into the twentieth century; four of them are preserved by the Nova Scotia Museum.

Shelburne

As the American Revolution was drawing to a close (1783 and after), 16,000 American settlers, including 2,000 Blacks loyal to the Crown, descended on Shelburne Harbour (then called Port Roseway) hoping to start a new life and create a town that would be as good or better than what they had left behind. They put all their energies into building a new urban centre with homes, stores, coffee houses, and even three newspapers. Unfortunately there was very little economic base to support their dreams. The soil was poor, making farming difficult. When their savings and government support ran out, the Loyalists left in bitter disappointment for Prince Edward Island, the Saint John River area of New Brunswick, other parts of Canada, England, and even the United States.

A few years after the population boom,

only 300 hardy souls remained. These were the ancestors of many of Shelburne's 2,250 citizens.

The wharves and boats are gone so it is hard to get a sense of life on the waterfront during the Loyalist period. But there is a palpable sense of time inside the buildings: we feel it at the tinkling of the spring bell as we enter the Ross-Thomson House and while kneeling in front of the huge basement fireplace where servants prepared meals. The Loyalists were cosmopolitan world-travellers. Their mantles were graced with elephant carvings from Burma and carpets from China.

The tourist bureau provides an excellent pamphlet titled "A Walking Tour of *Dock Street,* Shelburne: a Loyalist Town." It lists more *Shelburne* than thirty historic buildings and sites.

THE JOHN WILLIAMS DORY SHOP

On the waterfront is a museum from another era (1880–1971). In its heyday, The John Williams Dory Shop employed six men and built 350 dories a year, and there were six more dory shops down the road. The vigorous market for dories existed because the saltbank schooners that fished off the Grand Banks each used a dozen of the sturdy craft and a crew of about twenty to handline for fish. Today the large doors of the wood shop are open to the street and visitors can watch dories being made. Until 1993 veteran shipwright Sidney Mahaney built dory after dory in this shop ("ten hours a day, six days a week, all his working life; some say building 10,000 dories," including a model dory for Prince William). Now the shop is a testimonial not only to an old way of doing things but also a way of life gone with Mr. Mahaney.

THE ISLANDS PROVINCIAL PARK

DIRECTIONS:

Leave Shelburne on Route 3 west. Cross the Roseway River and proceed approximately 2 kilometres (1.2 miles) toward Birchtown. Turn left on the Barrack Cove Road and follow the signs to the park.

The Islands Provincial Park (for both picnicking and camping) is another green respite for travellers driving Route 103. It's just a few minutes off the highway at Exit 26, over a green one-lane bridge that spans the tea-coloured Roseway River, down a shady lane to the park at the head of Shelburne Harbour. Sheltered picnic tables are nestled close to the lapping water, and we enjoy a beautiful view of the town's skyline across the harbour. Huge white rocks spot the water's edge. Taking the lead from the birds we venture out on them.

BIRCHTOWN

Birchtown is 4 kilometers (2.5 miles) west of Shelburne on Route 3 (from Route 103 take Exit 27).

Imagine Shelburne Harbour to be the silhouette of an arm and the top of the harbour to be a hand clenched in a two fingered "V for Victory" sign. The Loyalist town of Shelburne was settled on the eastern finger while the western finger was set aside for the "Black Loyalists." The year 1784 was a full eighty-two years before the Thirteenth Amendment, which abolished slavery in the United States.

In order to lure away support for the revolutionaries in the Thirteen Colonies, British officials promised freedom to any slave who would fight on their side. After they lost the war, this promise could only be kept by transporting the Blacks to other British colonies. While other Loyalists had a hard time making a go of it and all but abandoned the place within a few years, the life of the Black Loyalists was far more grim. Most of them left as well. One large group sailed away in 1792 to a new colony in Sierra Leone, Africa.

Some families did struggle and survive. Certainly they would have rather stayed here than return to the United States and slavery. Genealogists will find their descendants amongst such family names of as James, Bennett, Barry, Herbert, Stevens, Cromwell, Jacklin, Matthew, and others.

Little physical evidence has survived of the Black community. A group of dedicated volunteers, however, has succeeded in having Birchtown—the Black community—declared an historic site. The local Anglican Church (circa 1904–06) is being renovated as a museum and an archaeological dig is an ongoing project. To date they have uncovered a 2.75 metre x 2.75 metre (9-foot x 9-foot) dwelling that has been described as being "similar to slave houses of the late 1700s in Virginia".

The Shelburne County Museum has documents and artifacts of the Black Loyalist community, including the muster book of the Free Black settlement and an ambrotype of Maria Blue, a prominent citizen of Birchtown.

BARRINGTON PASSAGE AREA

DIRECTIONS:

Leave Halifax on Route 103 west. Route 103 ends in Barrington and resumes at Oak Park. At Barrington, continue east on Route 3 to Barrington Passage.

Leave Yarmouth on Route 103 east. Take Exit 31 at Pubnico and follow Route 3 east to Barrington Passage

SAND HILLS BEACH PROVINCIAL PARK

Sand Hills Beach Provincial Park at Villagedale is only 6 kilometres (4 miles) south of Route 103 (Exit 29) and a good place to stop for a picnic and, weather willing, a swim. (There are public showers to wash off the salt water.) We follow the boardwalk, built to protect the fragile shore-line down to the "Sand Hills"—huge white sand dunes behind the beach. Here is lovely Barrington Bay. We imagine that these white hills were a beacon for ships. There is some controversy about whether a French fort (Fort Sainte-Louis) stood on this site. Some point to traces of a star-shaped granite foundation and apple trees that they believe to be descendants of trees planted by Acadians who were driven from the Sand Hills in 1756.

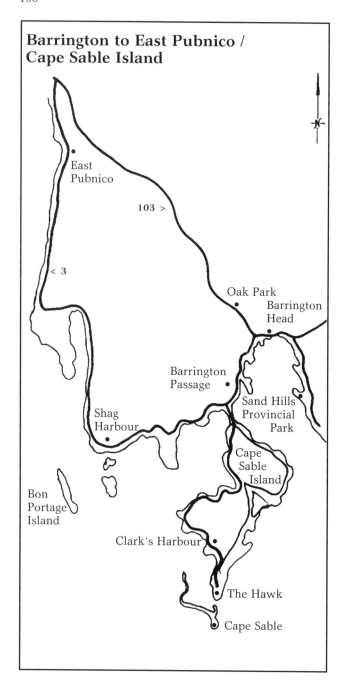

Barrington to East Pubnico / Cape Sable Island

East
Pubnico

103 >

< 3

Oak Park
Barrington
Head

Barrington
Passage

Sand Hills
Provincial
Park

Shag
Harbour

Cape
Sable
Island

Bon
Portage
Island

Clark's Harbour

The Hawk

Cape Sable

BARRINGTON WOOLLEN MILL

The Barrington River is a lively babbling stream; it's grassy bank invites a picnic. A hundred years ago the river was valued as a powerful resource. Residents built a dam and allowed the water to flow only through carefully regulated flumes. They sunk a vertical shaft water wheel into the flow and connected it by belts and wheels to harness machines that could work 100 times faster than men and women. These complex carding, spinning, and weaving machines were run by capturing a clean natural resource until just thirty-five years ago. (The mill operated from 1882–1962.)

In 1966 this last remaining water-powered woollen mill in Eastern Canada was on the verge of being dismantled and shipped to a textile museum in the States. The Cape

Sable Historical Society petitioned the government, and in 1968 the Barrington Woollen Mill became part of the Nova Scotia Museum, managed by the Historical Society.

Barrington Woollen Mill, Barrington

BARRINGTON MEETING HOUSE

Across the street, at a sharp turn in the road, is the Barrington Meetinghouse. It was built in 1765 as the focal point of a community made up of forty families from Cape Cod who had been granted 40,486 hectares (100,000 acres) at the head of Barrington Bay. Their life centred around the harbour and the river. The Meetinghouse was built by a local ship-wright, Joshua Nickerson, and his boatbuilding skill can be seen in the ship's knees (braces) that strengthen the roof. Because there were no sawmills at the time and the residents lived in log cabins, it is believed that the oak frame and .61-metre-wide (2-foot-wide) sawn boards came from New England. The pews were framed with boxes that segregated rich from poor and probably kept families close together for warmth in winter. We appreciate the simple lines of the structure.

There is a tiny burying ground behind the Meetinghouse.

We are touched by one stone that reads: *Here lies the body of Mrs. Lettice Doane, wife of Mr. Thomas Doane. She died in chield berth and was buried with her chield in her armes. July 26, 1766, age 30 years.*

SEAL ISLAND LIGHTHOUSE MUSEUM

Travellers on the Lighthouse Route are sometimes disappointed by the scarcity of lighthouses along the main road. They shouldn't be surprised: lighthouses by their very nature belong on god-forsaken rocky shoals. But here's the next best thing, the Seal Island Light Museum right on Route 3 in the village of Barrington Passage. It's not on an island, nor is it a working lighthouse, but it is indeed the lantern from the Seal Island Lighthouse. This revolving beacon (circa 1902), manufactured in Paris, France, has been mounted on a 10.7 metre (35-foot) base. The actual lighthouse was 20.4 metres (67 feet) high. We climb the sixty-six stairs up into the warmth of the greenhouse-like lantern, inspecting the hand-operated mechanism along the way. What a tedious job it must have been to keep this thing lit!

On the wall is a neatly framed document: Directions for Lighthouse Keepers under the Jurisdiction of the Government of Canada. There are thirty-five rules listed. Number one states the obvious: "Light the light punctually every day at sunset and extinguish it at sunrise."

Our favourite rule is number thirty-four. "These instructions are to be carefully preserved and the keeper is required to make himself perfectly acquainted with them."

This lighthouse was saved by a community effort that lobbied government. Why would the people go to so much trouble? Because Seal Island has a tremendous emotional resonance for people in the area. Less than one-quarter the size of the infamous "graveyard of the Atlantic," Sable Island, Seal Island has had a comparable number of wrecks. The spars of numerous old ships, chopped up like so many matchsticks, have littered its shores. In 1979 the complicated operating mechanism and lantern were dismantled and transported by helicopter.

Seal Island Light Museum, Barrington

THE ROMANCE AND REALITY OF LIGHTHOUSES

Seal Island is 27.6 kilometres (20 miles) off the coast of Clark's Harbour, at the elbow of the Fundy inlet where tides are the highest in the world. If there ever was a need for a bright flame to warn mariners it is here. Since the first lighthouse was built here in 1830, 120 ships have been lost. How many went aground before it was built? How many more would have gone aground without it? A modern signal that flashes a warning 22 kilometres (16 miles) in all directions has replaced the relic in Barrington. A droning foghorn does double duty.

In her book *Down in Nova Scotia,* Clara Dennis gives an account of an extraordinary visit to Seal Island in 1934. She had dinner with the lighthouse keeper's family and describes the dishes, retrieved from shipwrecked vessels.

"A cup came out of the *Snipe,* a beam trawler which was wrecked on Limb's Limb; the exceptionally pretty platter came out of the ill-fated *Columbia,* which struck in thick fog on Black Ledges ninety years ago."

The knives and forks were stamped with "Diamond Jubilee" from a steamer loaded with Queen Victoria's diamond jubilee mementos. (The crew of sixty-three was saved.) The chair she sat on came from one wreck, the table from another.

As a kind of macabre spring ritual, fishermen would visit the islands to bury the dead—bodies that washed up and those who had perished after dragging themselves upon the uninhabited islands. They also collected whatever cargo had washed up on the shore.

The salvaging and stripping of wrecks was a profitable business. When a ship ran aground, all boats available headed out. "Wrackers" collected little boys' sailor suits, carpets, bolts of satin, furniture, machinery—whatever was on board. There was a summer when all the women and girls of one community flaunted imported silk parasols.

CAPE SABLE

DIRECTIONS:

At Barrington Passage take Route 330 south across the causeway to Cape Sable Island. Follow Route 330 south to Centreville, Clark's Harbour, and The Hawk.

Place names in this region are somewhat confusing. According to the topographic map, solid ground and water have the same name. Leaving behind the village of Barrington Passage, we cross the crushed-rock causeway and notice that the body of water we're passing here is also called Barrington Passage. We drive onto an island named Cape Sable Island, according to our map; but to the residents it's Cape Island. No problem. After all, we've heard of the famous Cape Island boat. But then there's another island at the southern tip of Cape Sable Island (actually a sand spit with a magnificent lighthouse) called Cape Sable. All of this of course is not to be confused with the notorious Sable Island, which is another story entirely.

The 1.4 kilometre (one-mile-long) causeway we take for granted was built to replace ferry boats of the past. Originally passengers traversed the passage on sailing skiffs that were replaced by rowboats, then steamboats, and finally diesel-powered boats. In 1949, amidst a lot of fanfare, Premier Angus L. MacDonald cut a ribbon to open the causeway while schools of confused mackerel circled around not quite sure which way to go.

Cape Sable is as good as its name. (Sable means sand in French.) It is blessed with a glorious 6.9-kilometre-long (5-mile-long) beach on its southeastern side. Access to the beach is at The Hawk, South Side, and Stoney Island. Causeway Beach is a warmer and more sheltered stretch of sand that can be reached by turning right at the Corbett Heights Subdivision, just over the causeway.

We drive the complete loop of the island and on a summer's day the seascape is tranquil and glistening. All along the road, windows face the sea, anticipating the welcome sight of returning fishermen. This island, especially Clark's Harbour, has always been about fish and boats.

At the southern tip of the island we turn right on Hawk Road. We're very close to sea level, and it doesn't take much imagination to see that this low-lying land could easily be swallowed up in a gale. Dehydrated splatters of rockweed indicate the extent of last winter's fury. Beyond the fish plant, the lobster pound, and the shallow sandy channel, an elegant sentinel rises out the rocks—the Cape Sable Light. It would be easy to run aground here and the beacon is essential. The white light flashes every five seconds and is visible for 40.6 kilometres (29.5 miles).

Cape Sable is the most southerly point on Canada's Atlantic coastline. This island was marked on the earliest maps of the New World. (Cap du Sable is on the Sieur de

Lalanne's 1684 map of Acadia.) Before
modern navigational aids, most ships sailing
between Europe and the United States took
bearings from Cape Sable.

Looking for the beach we turn back on
the Hawk Road, take a loop to the right and
park behind a huge heaped-up wall of rock.
Clambering up, slipping back down the pile,
we finally reach the top and are rewarded
with a most extraordinary sight visible only at
low tide. It is beyond the angry tangle of driftwood, trap remnants, fishermen's gloves, and
"deadman's fingers" sponges tossed up by the
most recent ocean tumult. Below the rock
barrier, seemingly growing out of the sand, is
what is left of a forest—now just stumps and
roots rising askew out of the salt water. We
approach with a strange feeling of reverence.
These trees have been dead for 1,500 years,
drowned by a rising sea and ironically preserved by the same salty force that killed
them. They are rock hard to the touch and are
surrounded by chunks of dark peaty soil that
once nourished them. Somehow they don't
feel like they belong in our time.

THE CAPE ISLAND BOAT

The Cape Island boat, the workhorse of the
inshore fishery fleet, was first designed and
built here in 1907 by Ephraim Atkinson. At
the turn of the century, when fishermen
were converting from wind and sail power
to gas engine propulsion they found the traditional schooner designs inefficient.
Atkinson designed a boat to complement the
motor. It had a distinctive high bow, a shallow bottom, and a broad, open workspace.
This boat has survived the test of time and is

known today for its speed, economy, and safety.

A museum in Centreville on Cape Sable is named after an early settler, Archelaus Smith, who came from Chatham, Massachusetts in 1773. It features local history and displays relating to the lobster fishing and shipbuilding industries.

BARRINGTON TO EAST PUBNICO/ EAST PUBNICO TO BARRINGTON

DIRECTIONS:
Leave Halifax on Route 103 west. Route 103 ends in Barrington and resumes at Oak Park. At Barrington continue east on Route 3 through Barrington Passage and Woods Harbour to Route 103 at Pubnico.

Leave Yarmouth on Route 103 east. Take Exit 31 at Pubnico. Follow Route 3 east through the Pubnicos, through Woods Harbour to Barrington Passage.

This road is a real marine drive. Rarely does it veer away from the water including: Barrington Passage, Cockerwit Passage, Woods Harbour, and finally Pubnico Harbour. This is the unspoiled domain of fishermen and the sea on which they make their living. Just as the fog can lock fishermen in for days at a time, so it has a similar effect on the travelling public. As scenic as the road is when the visibility is good, we do not recommend that anyone venture down it on a day of seething grey mists. There may be water out there, but it might as well be sky.

Shag Harbour (the harbour not the town) is full of little islands. Some are just specks on

the map with descriptive names that arouse
our curiosity about their christening:
Deadmans Island, Grannies Brunt, and the
Rat. The larger islands are Inner Island,
Stoddart Island, and Outer Island (which used
to be called Bon Portage Island).

EVELYN M. RICHARDSON

Evelyn M. Richardson and her husband
Morrill Richardson owned Bon Portage, a
263-hectare (650-acre) island where they
were the lighthouse-keepers from 1926 until
1961 when they retired to Barrington. Evelyn
M. Richardson re-created the life of a
lightkeeper's family in her book *We Keep a
Light,* which won the Governor General's
Award for creative non-fiction in 1945. This
warm account of the romance and isolation
of island life was a balm to readers weary of
international strife at the end of the Second
World War. The book is still in print today.
In the town of Shag Harbour the elementary
school has been named in her honour. Bon
Portage was deeded by the family to Acadia
University in Wolfville to be used as a nature
sanctuary.

The observation tower of the Chapel Hill
Museum in Shag Harbour is the best place to
see the lighthouses of Bon Portage, West
Head, Cape Sable, and Seal Island as well as
much of Cape Sable Island.

Evelyn Richardson describes a similar
view *In We Keep a Light.*

*This hour of "lighting up" is a time that I
enjoy. I love to watch the beams of near-by lights
take their places like friendly stars in the twi-
light. Though I know only one of the keepers, the
lights themselves are old friends. Off there, about*

*twelve miles to the west, is Seal Island's rather
irregular beam; to the south-west is nothing but
unbroken sea and sky, but eight miles to the
south-east is Cape Sable's bright white flash; not
so far away and almost due east glows West
Head's warm red; while nearest to us, only two
miles away, is the twinkling little harbour light
of Emerald Isle. Then to the north, snug and protected by the outlying capes and islands, the
small fixed light of Wood's Harbour glows redly.*

Photographs and articles from the life
of Evelyn Richardson are on display in the
museum.

Also of interest are Gilbert Nickerson's
famous "wreckwood" chairs. A kindly old
gentleman who lived his life in Shag Harbour,
Nickerson had a hobby of collecting wood
from shipwrecks. What to do with the pieces?
He built chairs. Starting with a fragment of a
brigantine that had gone down off Cape Sable,
he had scraps from Kaiser Wilhelm's private
yacht, the American warship *Constitution*
(circa 1797), and the *North Star* (wrecked near
Yarmouth in 1919). He was given a piece of
wood found amongst the bodies from the
wreck of all wrecks—the *Titanic*. He carved
out a small leaf and tacked it on as a final de-
tail to one of his chairs.

BEACH POINT LIGHT

Just across the Shelburne/Yarmouth County line a small road appears on the left. The sign reads "Lighthouse Road to Beach Point" and since we can't resist a lighthouse we head down the .15 kilometre (1/4-mile) stretch to a storm-tossed rubble bulwark and a vigorous surf. The beach is covered with the kind flotsam and jetsam prized by beachcombers. We salvage a heap of rope (to be untangled much later in front of a winter fire) and a wooden lobster crate ideal for storing kindling. The rocks are ingrained with intriguing swirl-patterns, indicating that they were born of volcanic fire. The nature of their existence today is still violent, but their adversary now is water. The rocks are driven onto the beach along with our tangle of rope. Roaring air trapped between the rocks delights us. So does the eerily melodic foghorn. The fog is so thick we cannot see the light. In these vague mists it sounds not unlike the alien call in *Close Encounters of the Third Kind.*

WEST PUBNICO TO ARCADIA

Travelling the roads of Argyle we get the inaccurate impression that the communities here are far apart. In fact they're quite close to each other, by boat.

This is an area where a crow's view of things would really help. It's easy enough to get a sense of place from the ground if the land is reasonably flat and the roads have been laid out in a grid-like pattern. But it's a different matter when dozens of fingers of land are separated by briny inlets and a scatter of islands. The southeastern half of Yarmouth County can be geographically confusing because while most of mainland Nova Scotia has been settled on an east-west axis (we travel from Halifax to Yarmouth, for example), the natural lay of the land here is north to south. The great underlying structure of bedrock settled this way and glaciers scoured away the softer materials leaving a series of long parallel ridges and valleys. Finally the ocean rose and crept up the valleys filling them with sea water.

Side roads hang down from the main high-way (Route 3) like the feeder roots of a tree. Our choices are numerous and tantalizing, but every time we explore a peninsula we have to retrace our steps in order to continue our trip.

Cape Island fishing boats, Pubnico

Between Argyle, Ste. Anne du Ruisseau, and Tusket, the landscape is peaceful and un-hurried. Estuarine water flows, but not too swiftly. Sheltered inlets allow marsh grasses to grow, providing resting and feeding places for waterfowl. Black ducks, Canada geese, scaups, and common goldeneye thrive in the marshland. Osprey and bald eagles are also abundant.

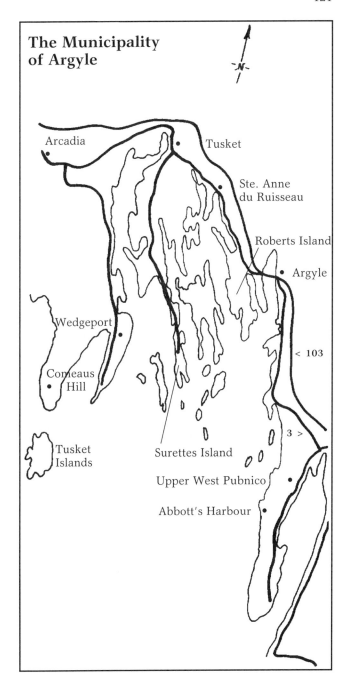

The Municipality of Argyle

Arcadia

Tusket

Ste. Anne du Ruisseau

Roberts Island

Argyle

Wedgeport

< 103

Comeaus Hill

3 >

Tusket Islands

Surettes Island

Upper West Pubnico

Abbott's Harbour

YARMOUTH COUNTY

As we drive further down the peninsulas, and farther out to sea, the climate and landscape become increasingly more restless.

At the very end of road are places such as Chebogue Point, Pinkneys Point, Comeaus Hill, and the Wedge Point, which offer striking views of the Gulf of Maine and the Tusket Islands. These islands used to bustle with activity when the commercial and sport fisheries were vital. Now they are mostly the seasonal domain of lobster fishermen and hunters. Someday we will drive down to Little River Harbour and ask a fisherman to take us out to see the islands close up.

Sign on Route 103

The highway sign reads, "Oldest Community still Acadian." From Pubnico to Comeaus Hill a dozen or so names dominate the mailboxes: Amirault, Babin, Belliveau, Boudreau, Bourque, Cottreau, D'Eon, Doucette, D'Entremont, Jacquard, Landry, LeBlanc, Muise, Pothier, Surette. Some of these people are direct descendants of a unique group of Acadians whose history reads a little differently from the other "neutral French" of Grand Pré, Port Royal, and

Beaubassin. Because the French settlers of Pubnico (or Pombomcoup as it was originally called in 1653) lived in a less densely populated area, they were the last to be rounded up and deported in the *Grand Dérangement* (Great Upheaval).

They were also the first to return. After ten years in exile in New England, the d'Entremonts, Miuses, and Amiraults sailed back to the same area they had left. They were unlike other Acadians whose rich farmland (in the Annapolis and Saint John River valleys) had been supplanted by British ex-military and New England Planters. Acadians from other parts of N.S. were eventually granted land in the Pubnico area as well.

WEST PUBNICO

West Pubnico, like many of the other villages in Argyle, is a quiet, neat, close-knit, and very proudly Acadian community. Signs are bilingual. We stop by D'Eon's Bakery for some cake doughnuts and "rappie pie" (to heat up later). This traditional Southwest Nova Scotian casserole is made with a vat of grated potatoes, squeezed dry of starchy water, simmered in a pot of fragrant broth (such as quahog clam or chicken), and baked forever until crusty on the outside and gooey on the inside. Rappie pie is served at local restaurants and at "the Acadian Festival," a major community event that takes place here mid-summer.

Musée Acadien (the Acadian Museum) opposite the fire station is an old Acadian home (circa 1864) featuring a collection of domestic articles and memorabilia donated by the community. Of interest to genealogists are old maps and the first land grants, from the 1700s.

The settlement is on the sheltered side of the Pubnico peninsula. The more tempestuous western shore (called Lobster Bay) can be experienced at Abbotts Harbour where there is a lighthouse, a picnic park, and more open sea.

The British army burned almost everything after wrenching the Acadians from their homes, so very little physical evidence of their lives has survived. One exception is the mill stones at Middle West Pubnico. They used to grind grain at what is now Downey Brook at Brass Hill, Shelburne County. After the expulsion they were moved to Ryders Brook Mill in Central Argyle, but were eventually returned to the descendants of the original owners who presently live in West Pubnico. In 1965, these rare examples of the Acadian heritage, literal touchstones for the people, were put on display near the Red Cap restaurant.

Roberts Island a little farther along Route 3 has an intriguing history. A group of Acadian men were interred there, awaiting deportation. At low tide, some of the prisoners escaped across the flats and the island acquired the ironic nickname *Ile Non-Parison* (meaning Non-Prisoner Island).

Glenwood Provincial Park, close to the Route 103, is a good place for a break. It is insulated from the 100 kilometre-per-hour (60 mile-per-hour) speedway by a pretty wood on tiny Rickers Lake.

SAINTE-ANNE'S CATHOLIC CHURCH

Sainte-Anne's Catholic Church at Ste. Anne du Ruisseau rises high out of the salt marsh where generations ago Acadians built sod barricades to stem the tide and transform water into arable land. The imposing turn-of-the-century white and black trimmed wooden structure is the pride of the community. The grounds and gothic-style rectory next door are meticulously kept. Travellers are welcomed inside to view the ornate vaulted ceilings and expanses of polished wood.

This church is a grand place of worship, but it has very old and humble beginnings. The parish is the oldest in the region. We follow a road beside the church to Rocco Point where a log cabin chapel was built in 1784 by Acadians who had returned after the expulsion. The chapel is long gone but we can imagine how joyful the deportees must have been to return to this place and rebuild their homes and church.

We follow the road down to a wharf on a gentle bay called the Little Sluice. In 1799 Abbé Jean Mande Sigogne stepped ashore here from a fishing schooner. Exiled during the French Revolution, he had come to the New World to start a new life. He became the spiritual leader of the revived community and built a church which was the spiritual predecessor of the current Sainte-Anne's.

Sainte-Anne's Catholic Church

TUSKET/OLD COURTHOUSE

Along this sparsely populated pastoral drive we are pleasantly surprised to come upon Tusket, a small cluster of rather stately old homes. In the 1860s six bustling shipyards were situated on the now quiet banks of the Tusket River. This community was founded in 1784 by Dutch United Empire Loyalists from New York and New Jersey. They brought with them a strong sense of law and justice, and in 1804 they built a courthouse that is now a museum. The Argyle Township Court and Gaol is the oldest standing courthouse in Canada.

Across the road from the courthouse is a parking lot next to the river. It serves also as a launching point for canoes. The Tusket River on both sides of Route 103 is very popular with canoeing enthusiasts.

On our way from Amiraults Hill to Surettes Island we cross a narrow passageway called the Indian Sluice. Here we witness the staggering power of the converging tides. The iron bridge crossing the channel was built in 1909 and considered a great engineering feat at the time, having been built upriver and floated into place on the rushing tide.

MARIE BABIN SURETTE

On Surettes Island we find the grave of Marie Babin Surette. Her headstone states that she died at age 110 on December 8, 1862, and that she was the last survivor of the Acadian deportation of 1755. We do a quick calculation (she'd have been three) and are skeptical about her having survived eleven decades, but we feel immediately ashamed. Here lies the namesake of this island, the progenitor of many of its residents. At the very least she was a channel for the stories of her parents and grandparents. They must have vowed, as they mourned from the decks of crowded ships, that they would never forget the agony of being rounded up like cattle, torn from their loved ones, and made to witness unspeakable horrors. Whether or not she herself was uprooted as a baby, Marie Babin Surette would have listened to these stories so agonizingly real that she felt like she had lived them herself.

At Arcadia a nature trail has been blazed behind the elementary school. It's called the Utkubok Trail and features interpretive stations that describe twelve distinct wildlife habitats. It's wheelchair and stroller accessible with assistance.

YARMOUTH

DIRECTIONS:

Leave Halifax on Route 103 west. Follow Route 103 to its end at the Hardscratch Road. Turn left at Hardscratch Road, then right on Starrs Road. Turn left on Main Street to reach the town centre and ferries to the United States.

SHOPPING DOWNTOWN MAIN STREET

Like so many towns in North America, Yarmouth spreads out for miles, with automobile-accomodating malls, fast food, and franchise stores. But when the ferries dock and passengers flow through downtown Yarmouth it still bristles like a real seaport. Main Street has a turn-of-the-century feel. Its

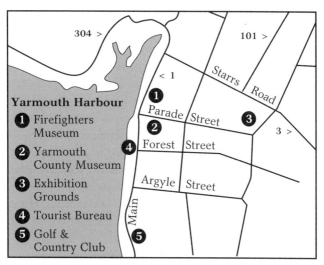

Yarmouth Harbour

1. Firefighters Museum
2. Yarmouth County Museum
3. Exhibition Grounds
4. Tourist Bureau
5. Golf & Country Club

Yarmouth

The Horse Fountain, Yarmouth

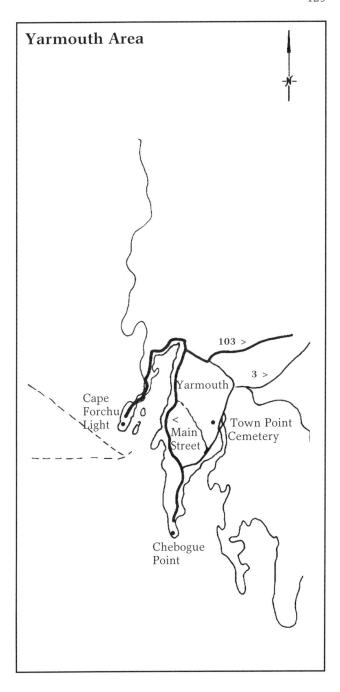

Yarmouth Area

N

103 >

3 >

Yarmouth

Cape
Forchu
Light

Town Point
Cemetery

<
Main
Street

Chebogue
Point

many red-brick facades were built when the proud motto of the newly incorporated town was "Progress." Today the downtown is again on the upswing. Window shopping is varied, as you'd expect in what's effectively a border town. During tourist season, when a majestic blow from the ship's horn resounds through Yarmouth, everyone knows that hordes of energetic shoppers are close behind.

The shops are one-of-a-kind, owner-run, and many cater to tourists. The Yarmouth Wool Shoppe features everything Scottish, from tartans and books about them to Burberry tweeds. There are souvenir shops galore selling trinkets, baubles, gewgaws, and chotchkes. Every store has its own personality: the carnival atmosphere of Mr. Leonard's ("You can wear our sweaters but you can't wear them out"), the historic ambiance of R. H. Davis and Co. (third generation of Davises to mind the store), and the Shop of the Christmas Elves that believes in celebrating Christmas twelve months of the year. Interspersed amongst such colourful establishments are the shops that cater to the daily needs of residents featuring shoes, furniture, and clothing.

Tiny Frost Park on the harbour side of Main Street (between Public Street and Glebe Street, across from the Western Counties Regional Library) is a delightful Victorian-flavoured respite for weary shoppers. Fronted with wrought-iron fencing and a gazebo, its centrepiece is a three-tiered old-fashioned fountain. As the water splashes down from dish to dish we overhear a conversation between two children about to toss their pennies into the water. Their talk concerns the timing of the wish. Is it proper

Main Street,
Yarmouth

to wish the wish before throwing the coin,
while it's in midair, or after it hits the
water?

Just up from Main Street (about eight
blocks from Parade to Albert) we are as-
tounded to discover Yarmouth's grand
neighbourhood. Here are dozens of spacious
and ornately decorated homes: Gothic revival,
Queen Anne, Georgian, Second Empire,
Italianate style houses with widow's walks,
pilasters, towers, gingerbread, and arches.
They were built by Yarmouth's sea captains,
shipping magnates, and industrialists in the
late 1800s. (Prominent family names of the day
included Killam, Baker, Lewis, Robbins, Cann,

Moody, Burrill, and Lovitt.) If something could
be embellished or bedecked, it was.

The money to create this grandeur came
from shipping. Yarmouth's ships carried local
lumber and salt fish to the Caribbean, where
they traded their cargo for rum, sugar, and
molasses. On their way back to Yarmouth
they stopped in Boston to trade some of it and
to pick up manufactured goods.

Later, trading became much more complex, as Yarmouth's ships served the world
carrying whatever needed to be transported—
coal from Great Britain to the West Indies or
timber from the St. Lawrence to South
America. At the height of its mercantile success, the late 1800s, Yarmouth was the second
largest port of registry after Saint John, N.B.
(229 vessels with a total tonnage of 118,000).

YARMOUTH COUNTY MUSEUM

The Yarmouth County Museum at 22 Collins
Street documents the great shipping age with
more than eighty oil paintings of ships
owned or commanded by Yarmouth citizens.
Other nautical artifacts include models,
booty from shipwrecks, and the original lens
from the old Cape Forchu Light (circa 1840).
It was designed by French physicist Augustin
Jean Fresnel who devised a method of producing circularly polarized light, thus replac-
ing mirrors with compound lenses. The lens
had 360 prisms, weighed 1,495 kilograms
(3,300 pounds), and cost $38,000—a fortune
at the time.

Down the road from the ferry terminal at
90 Water Street is the Killam Brothers Shipping Office. Part of the waterfront revitaliza-
tion plan, it is now a museum where visitors

can get a feel for the shipping business as it operated around the turn of the century.

A well-illustrated pamphlet titled *A Walking Tour of Yarmouth* is available at the tourist bureau. It outlines a self-guided tour through the commercial and domestic sections of town. We note that there are also organized guided bus tours offered to visitors.

FIREFIGHTERS' MUSEUM OF NOVA SCOTIA

We have children with us so we are grateful that one fire engine has been singled out for its kid-proof qualities. It's a big, red, and very sturdy 1935 Bickle that has been donated by the Mill Village Fire Department. Presently, the steering wheel is under the control of a small wild child whose imagination has him careening all over the road on the way to an inferno. We are a bit dismayed at the sign on the truck forbidding grown-ups to join in the fun. Who hasn't dreamed of riding a shiny red fire truck at top speed with screeching sirens?

This display of machinery is all about the romance of a very specialized kind of technology. Here it is all lovingly painted, polished, and maintained: chrome bumpers of steam pumpers, copper boilers, hoses, and wooden-spoked wheels. One horse-drawn engine, the Ronald steamer (circa 1890), weighs 2,265 kilograms (5,000 pounds). It must have been quite a team of horses that pulled that one amongst the heat, smoke, and confusion of a fire.

Sobering photographs upstairs give us insight into the purpose of all this impressive machinery. Fire trucks were designed to save wooden structures. Many of the old wood-framed, wood-roofed, wood-shingled buildings were lovely, but they were also firetraps. We don't think about fire as much as they used to at the turn of the century, when a whole downtown could be razed overnight as happened in Bridgewater. The threat of forest fire doesn't seem to be as much of a spectre as it was even in 1955 when fire destroyed 2,834 hectares (7,000 acres) of forest and licked at the edges of the town of Liverpool.

No wonder firefighting equipment is treated with respect bordering on veneration.

YARMOUTH TO CHEBOGUE

DIRECTIONS:
From the Yarmouth town centre follow Main Street south through Sand Beach and Kelly Cove. At Rockville turn right on the Chebogue Point Road. When leaving Chebogue Point turn right at Rockville. Proceed east to Town Point to the cemetary. Return to Yarmouth through Central Chebogue and Arcadia.

This drive is a day's scenic excursion for travellers staying in Yarmouth. It offers a study in contrasts. Leaving downtown Yarmouth, we travel south on Main Street along the edge of Yarmouth Sound (from where there's a good view of Cape Forchu) through the stark landscape of Kelly Cove. Lashed by storms and not blessed with hospitable soil conditions, life has been hard here for anyone trying to make a living from the land. By contrast, the western side of the Chebogue Peninsula is semi-agricultural, doubly blessed with a serene estuary and decent growing conditions.

At Rockville there is a dead-end road to Chebogue Point, which is an irresistible invitation to see what's at the end of it. Along the way there are spectacular views of gravel spits, reefs, and islands. The headlands are abrupt and taper off into the sea. We can see islands in violent transition and wonder where they will end up, when the surf has finished sorting them out. Perhaps they will wash up on the sand beach at Cape Forchu?

THE TOWN POINT CEMETERY

The Town Point Cemetery at Chebogue is so named because this was where the town of Yarmouth was supposed to have been built. In 1767 the township of Yarmouth was created on paper in Halifax by a stroke of the pen of Governor Lawrence. It stretched from "Cape Fourchu to the River Tuskett." But when the settlers arrived, they found the sheltered area east of the Sound more hospitable and settled there instead.

For travellers who've never considered exploring a cemetery, this is a good place to start. Cherished for generations, it is a provincially registered heritage property, and is one of the most serene landscapes in Nova Scotia. The cemetery is bounded by a gently moving estuary, the Chebogue River, on one side and a "dry stone wall" on the other. It is *dry* because the stones fit together with such precision that they have remained in place for a century or more without so much as a smattering of mortar.

On the stone wall a plaque reads, "This tablet commemorates the landing of the first

English-speaking settlers near this spot on June 9, 1761." That year the shallop *Pompey Dick* sailed into Chebogue River with the Ellis, Landers, and Perry families from Sandwich, Cape Cod.

There's still an emotional bond between Nova Scotia and "the Boston States." Etched into stone is one man's testimony to the beauty of this plot on the banks of the Chebogue River. Donald Browning Prentice was born in Providence, Rhode Island in November 23, 1907 and died there in March 8, 1984, but he chose to be laid to rest here. His tombstone reads,

> *"He loved this spot—*
> *With its landscapes and seascapes-*
> *The liquid clarity of its light and its colour*
> *all soft and caressing*
> *making a unity of earth and sea and sky."*

We ponder a white marble lady who reclines on a sheaf of wheat. This unusual scupture marks the grave of Margaret McNaught Webster, mother of ten, who died on August 27, 1864 at the age of forty-nine. She was the wife of Dr. Frederick Augustus Webster, the first doctor to practise in Yarmouth. The story goes that while studying medicine in Scotland he went for a stroll in the country and came upon Margaret, a young lass, asleep on a sheaf of wheat.

After his wife died Dr. Webster had this image of his love, as he first encountered her, carved into pure white Italian marble. Her funeral was held in Yarmouth and her coffin was taken by boat, accompanied by a procession of rowboats, around the Chebogue Point and up the channel of the river to her final resting place.

YARMOUTH TO CAPE FORCHU

DIRECTIONS:

From the Yarmouth town centre follow Main Street north to Vancouver Street. Turn left on Vancouver Street. Turn left on Route 304 to Overton. At Overton, turn left to Cape Forchu.

We ask for directions to Forchu..... "Drive down Main street and turn left at the horse fountain." What a curious thought. But sure enough there's a fountain and resplendent atop it is the sculpture of a golden horse. Unfortunately, water no longer gushes from the spouted mouths of the mythical fish for the benefit of thirsty travellers—both man and beast. In these modern times horses don't often pass by on their way to the Forchu Light.

On the other side of the harbour with a view of the Yarmouth skyline we discover a salt marsh where we're startled by half a dozen Canada geese taking flight. This is another side of Yarmouth's personality: a narrow peninsula of islands joined by sandbar/

Cape Forchu Light

breakwaters ending dramatically at the Cape Forchu Lighthouse.

At Yarmouth Bar, we pause between the heaving whitecaps of the Gulf of Maine on one side of the road and the more sheltered Yarmouth Sound on the other. The road snakes right through the middle of a fishing village. Thousands of lobster traps, both bent wooden and modern green mesh wire, are neatly stacked here in the off season. Almost every boat is a beauty—no fisherman seems content with just one shade of paint. Sublime and gaudy taste is expressed in combinations of red/purple/yellow and maroon/turquoise/pink.

There's a wooded knoll on Cape Forchu, a miniature cottage country, before we descend onto the last spit of land. We drive over False Harbour Beach where the sand keeps blowing on the road, past Footes Pond just as a great blue heron is rising up out of the bulrushes into the air.

Then the road just stops. Even on an early Sunday morning this a popular spot. The bedrock is marked with teenage graffiti (Class of '92, Wendy loves Andrew). The modern lighthouse looks like a cross between an apple core and a peppermint stick. But this is still a wild and craggy place. The paper-thin slate flakes off under our feet as we clamber over the rocks for a more dramatic view. This is the prime spot to watch ferries coming and going.

Barkhouse, Joyce. *A Name For Himself: a biography of Thomas Head Raddall.* Toronto: Irwin, 1986.

Compiling of the History of the Village of Chester 1759–1967. Chester Branch of W.I.N.S., 1967.

Cranston, Tony. *Disasters at Sea.* Yarmouth: Self-published, 1986.

Cunningham, Scott. *Coastal Paddling Routes in Nova Scotia.* Self-published, n.d.

Dawson, Joan. *The Mapmaker's Eye: Nova Scotia Through Early Maps.* Halifax: Nimbus and Nova Scotia Museum, 1988.

Dennis, Clara. *Down in Nova Scotia: My Own, My Native Land.* Toronto: The Ryerson Press, 1934.

DesBrisay, Mather Byles. *History of the County of Lunenburg.* Toronto: William Briggs, 1895. Facsimile edition: Mika, Belleville, 1972.

Erskine, John. *In Forest and Field.* Halifax: Nova Scotia Museum, 1976.

Fergusson, Charles Bruce. *Early Liverpool Diarist.* Halifax: Public Archives of N.S., 1961.

Fitch, Catherine et al. *Chester: a pictorial history of a Nova Scotia Village.* Toronto: Pagurian, 1983.

Grant, John N. *Black Nova Scotians.* Halifax: N.S. Museum, 1980.

Hamilton, William B. *The Nova Scotia Traveller.* Toronto: Macmillan, 1981.

Hichens, Walter W. *Island Trek (about Seal Island).* Hantsport: Lancelot, 1982.

Johnston, Helen Pauline. *Light on Evelyn Richardson.* Hantsport: Lancelot, 1975.

Johnson, Ralph S. *Forests of Nova Scotia.* Halifax: Department of Lands and Forests and Four East, 1986.

Kaulback, Ruth E. *Historic Saga of Leheve (LaHave).* Petite Rivière: Self-published, 1971.

Leefe, John. *The Atlantic Privateers.* Halifax: Petheric, 1978.

Livesay, J. F. B. *Peggy's Cove.* Toronto: The Ryerson Press, 1944.

Messenger, Margaret E. *Our Island Reminisces.* Cape Sable Island: the Archelaus Smith Historical Society, 1986.

Messenger, Margaret E. *Our Island's Bygone Days.* Cape Sable Island: the Archelaus Smith Historical Society, 1988.

Mills, Chris. *Vanishing Light: a lightkeeper's fascination with a disappearing way of life.* Hantsport: Lancelot, 1992.

Mitcham, Allison. *Paradise or Purgatory: island life in Nova Scotia and New Brunswick.* Hantsport: Lancelot, 1986.

More, James F. *The History of Queens County, N.S.* Halifax: Nova Scotia Printing Co., 1873. Facsimile edition: Mika, Belleville, 1972.

Norwood, Caroline B. *Life on the Tusket Islands.* Westport: Norwood Publishing, 1994.

Penney, Allen. *Houses of Nova Scotia: an illustrated guide to architectural-style recognition.* Halifax: Formac and the N.S. Museum, 1989.

Pentz, Donald R. *Risser's Beach Salt Marsh Trail.* Halifax: Department of Lands and Forests, n.d.

Perkins, Simeon. *The Diary of Simeon Perkins.* Toronto: The Champlain Society, 1961.

Perry, Hattie. *In and Around Old Barrington.* Self-published, 1979.

Perry, Hattie. *This was Barrington.* Self-published/N.S. Museum, 1973.

Plaskett, William. *Lunenburg: an inventory of historic buildings with photographs and historical and architectural notes.* Lunenburg County District Planning Commission, 1984.

Poole, Stephen. *Nova Scotia: a colour guidebook.* Halifax: Formac, 1994.

Pullen, Rear Admiral Hugh F. *The Sea Road to Halifax; being an account of the lights and buoys of Halifax Harbour.* Halifax: Maritime Museum of the Atlantic, 1980.

Raddall, Thomas H. *Ogomkegea: the story of Liverpool, N.S.* Liverpool: Queens County Museum, 1983. (Originally published 1934).

Richardson, E. M. *We Keep a Light.* Toronto: McGraw-Hill, 1945.

Ricker, Jackson. *Historical Sketches of Glenwood and the Argyles, Yarmouth County, N.S.* Halifax: McCurdy Print, 1941.

Roland, Albert E. *Geological Background and Physiography of Nova Scotia.* Halifax: Nova Scotia Museum, 1982.

Ross, Sally and Alphonse Deveau. *The Acadians of N.S.: past and present.* Halifax: Nimbus, 1992.

Smith, Eleanor Robertson, ed. *Lost Mariners of Shelburne County.* Shelburne County Genealogical Society, 1991.

South Shore; Seasoned Timber Volume 2: Some historic buildings from Nova Scotia's South Shore. Halifax: The Heritage Trust of Nova Scotia, 1974.

Stephens, David E. *Lighthouses of Nova Scotia.* Windsor: Lancelot Press, 1973.

Taylor, F. C. *Reconnaissance Geology of Shelburne Map-Area, Queens, Shelburne and Yarmouth Counties, Nova Scotia: Memoir 349.* Ottawa: Dept. of Energy, Mines and Resources Canada, 1964.

Tracy, Nicholas. *A Cruising Guide to the Bay of Fundy and the St. John River including Passamoquoddy Bay and the Southwestern Shore of Nova Scotia.* Fredericton: Goose Lane, 1992.

Trask, Deborah. *Life How Short, Eternity How Long: Gravestone Carving and Carvers in Nova Scotia.* Halifax: Nova Scotia Museum, 1978.

Withrow, Alfreda. *St. Margarets Bay: a history.* Seabright: Four East, 1985.

Woodworth, M. Marie. *The Early History of Port Mouton.* Liverpool: The Queens County Historical Society, 1983.

Yarmouth Once Upon a Time, 225 Yarmouth County Anniversary. Yarmouth: Town of Yarmouth/Municipality of Yarmouth, 1986.

Young, Alan R. *Thomas H. Raddall.* Boston: Twayne, 1983.